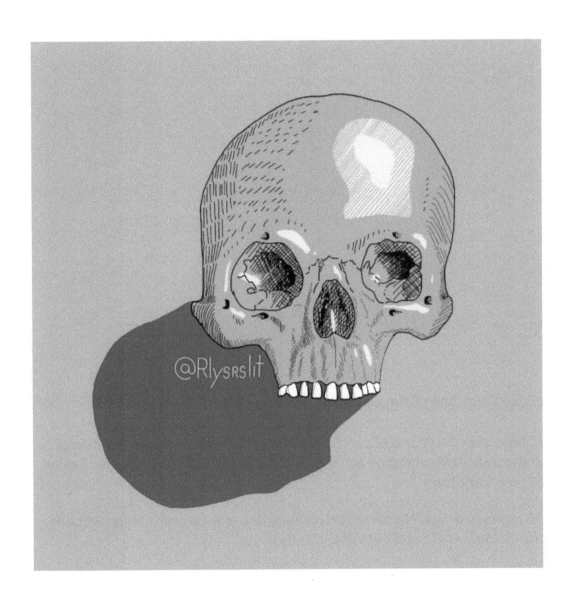
@Rlysʀslit

男友·视角
BOYFRIEND PERSPECTIVE

MICHAEL CHANG

YOU TOO SLIPPERY FOR ME / CAN'T HOLD YOU
LONG OR HARD.

Sonia Sanchez

YOU DON'T KNOW MY ATTRIBUTES / I HATE
YOU.

Alice Notley

NEW YORK REMEMBERING NIGHTS AWAKE

Everything in the city so commercial & drab

It needs more graffiti

U know mante religieuse is French for praying mantis, so elegant

Don't confuse my poivre for pauvre

No noble savages here

O'Hara may have written ~15 Jane poems but all my poems are abt u

Ur brand of hooligan-scholar, so hot

U make me cum just by existing

I think I saw u at the Mineshaft

I lit matches to mask the fecal smell

I was a long way from home, camp had no space for me

U invite absurd speculation

Ur bits, which delight us to see

It pains me to know there are parts of u I'm not able to access

That I'm not able to reach

I am deficient

It's extortion from all corners

I know u'll never sketch me, throw my initials on a wall

I love u just the same

I seek out ur throat, ur sound,

animals make noises in different languages

Ur navel, I plunge

7 days a week, sometimes twice a day

U are never underappreciated, a happy plant, regularly watered

U don't have to thank me (u never do)

We won't be that doomed couple, the ones who are "that way"

We are delicate, ambiguous

Certainty being the enemy of queerness

With u I feel immortal, my red-lipped saint

Be the Rivers to my O'Hara

Caveat I don't wanna die at 40

Let me make it to 50, at least a half-century, a number that has a cleanness to it

I've been dreaming of a house

Every night I roam the halls but I never find who I'm living with

The photos in this house are a blur, & the things in the closet are all mine

Still I'm left with the distinct impression that I'm not alone

It would be awful to be alone in such a big house, I think

Wasn't it Foucault who said there are many forms of silence?

& perhaps, as the Canadian contends, different ways of telling time …

Did u see what happened to her?

I think it was only a matter of time

With some ppl u can just tell they're a bad lay

From their poems, u mean? Lee Krasner didn't write poems

Franz Kline? Forget it

Make ur poetry interesting, go out, live ur life!

Ah, youthful abundance … it's a race to the bottom

I need my inhaler

COUGAR TOWN WIDOW CITY

"Last night I cried tears of joy / What did I do to deserve this?"—Rick Ross

The grand jury has returned an indictment
Gary Indiana—the man, not the place
When I look at my thin wrists
I can't help but think of some thick dick
I remember first becoming aware that I was talked abt,
with feverish zeal, just like sports
A football player in tight jeans, the way he filled out the front
Popular boys in shiny loafers they ordered thru the mail
Mifflintown or Millersville, who cares
Point is, boys want my muff, yearn to make it wink
Read me so filthy Sybill Trelawney
You can trust your life, trust where your process takes you
Maybe I want New England & mediocre
You tell me abt the lyric I & the abstract you
I say my Chinese face is poetic & my body is an awakening
I tell my students
Most of my poems are happy accidents
Follow your pleasures, write your obsessions
Listen to id, hear what it's telling you
Frat boys circling the wagons
Frat boys as desire machines
They desire desire desire
It's okay to want beauty beauty beauty
Encouragement is the best of all gifts
Respite close, "respite"—I've been saying that a lot
I've been majorly blah
I think I've realized you-know-who is fuckin bland & blah & whatever
My poet brain is dumb today
Baby bake me a cake
Tell me the habits of the petite bourgeoisie
Sign off on the plea agreement
How will you let freedom ring?
Everyone carries with them the capacity to wound, to disappoint
The sooner you realize that, the better off you'll be

You like them a little slow & long in the tooth
Undo
The last breath
The final gasp

CLAES & LITTLE BEAR (1990)

A boy named Gideon told me I was cute
But he only ate red M&Ms
& that is a crime

Why don't you understand
Why don't you get that
14th Street means something

A tomato sammich: respectable bread,
Blue Plate (Hellmann's if you're desperate),
& the best tomatoes you can find. Salt & pepper the mayo.
Boy says *that looks like something your bougie ass would eat.*

Pitbull says there's nothing like Miami's heat
Smokey Bear says only you can prevent forest fires
Yea write more abt the red-tailed hawk biatch

Startled by the size of your thing
limp as a boiled peanut
I find it ultimately unsatisfying

Idiosyncrasies of the intelligentsia
British boy doesn't know what a dugout is
I traffick in rumor & pocky

You think "cold stone" is poetic
I think cold stone is ice cream

I know not of power
nor of influence

I am but a simple writer
A humble scribe

I hope you won't mind
my undressing

Help yourself to white wine
some spaghetti & clams

PRAIRIE OYSTER

You can lie in poems
Lie perfectly still next to Grace Kelly—a woman named after a handbag
God don't like ugly
I don't think I had any real concept of college until after I got my doctorate
Then the expectations, the dreams, the wishes came
I used to hate the veneration of the basic
It just seemed so fake, so put on
Until I met Pat, who forwarded my mail even after I moved three times
The postal worker who toiled for decades & finally died on the job, shitting herself
Everyone is writing a memoir these days
Most ppl don't have anything interesting to say
So I have relaxed my standards
From today onward I will laud the basic
I won't foreclose any possibilities for my life or anybody else's
It's a Murakami trick—the narrator has a way of living
he thinks is totally normal & that everyone else thinks is strange
Like budae-jjigae, the spicy army stew, mouthwatering broth a colonial legacy
It's a miracle it's taken me this long to write a frat boy poem
Consider a gross sticky frat boy
Consider animal noises like blurguhugh
[uninterrupted grunting]
Consider how he uses my photos to catfish
Consider ppl secretly wanting exotic submissive Azns
Consider my playing along—I typed *alone* so yea alone too
Suppose I pee sitting down
Suppose I make him watch
Suppose he likes it
Report me to the EEOC, too bad fugly isn't a protected class
Funny how profs talk abt redheads (not a protected class)
Leave gingers alone
I have numbed my senses, I regard all emails with no emotion
When the locks fail & the dams do not hold
I want you posed just like that
One hand on the side of your face, meek & submissive
Like you're trying to recall Euripides
I read your mind, am comforted by your thoughts

or the thought of you nestled in my palm
Head thrown back
Throat to the stars
Inquisitive
& in a tizzy

SQUEEZE

There are two wolves, Dolce & Gabbana. First disarm them with a compliment, defuse their racist anger. Next summon whatever weapons you have in your arsenal, don't be shy. Then use every trick at your disposal, you are David & they are Goliath. Go in for the kill.

•

You dream of two kittens fighting. When you wake up, you realize that they were fighting over you, flinging themselves like ballerinas off a roof.

I dream I'm in a lecture hall. There is a stir because a white supremacist is in the room. I look over, see the swastika prominently tattooed onto his forehead. Everyone shifts, groaning, some ppl switch seats, & it feels good. I tell myself, performative allyship is better than no allyship, but it still maintains the odor & rot of a damp cloth. As much as I want to, I will not write a poem abt the Bearded Cuban, though I know him well.

Sometimes I feel like our relationship is two con artists trying to con one another. Then at some point in the scheme we realize we are both marks & make a hasty exit. It is messy yet delightful & utterly infuriating. I will dominate you, I will come back.

•

We are somewhere in my car, & you are hanging onto my every word arrectis auribus. You are so smart, so fluent in wanting, so proficient at radiating intelligence. I am radiating heat of a different kind.

We get physical, intestines around our necks, inflamed like the moon, ready to burst. You are a revelation, the type of boy used to being adored. I give approximately 3.5 years of my life to fuck you.

We are a story, meticulously plotted, but there is no neat ending, no bow to tie it all together. Fetch me a velvet bag, one of Tyrian purple, to keep the heart I have stolen from you.

•

For some reason I can't get over your square face, blunt features, how your face is kinda smushed together, the Devil's handiwork. You're as close to God as I'm gonna get. I don't want to be remembered as a genius, although I am, I want to be known as a hard worker.

Drown me in jizz, drench me in Welsh rarebit & condescension, drizzle me strawberry sauce, Japanese cheesecake soft, New York cheesecake hard, you succubus, you Knights Who Say Ni!

匪夷所思 UNBELIEVABLE ZUIHITSU

A hot coltish boy with two rows of teeth, a sensible twist on vagina dentata, it means his smile is visually interesting & he gets through his pastrami twice as quick.

There was a time when all we could talk abt was Bullshot Book Club, combining our two favorite things, beef broth & vodka. We fantasized abt Warhol stalking the aisles at Gristedes for canned soup, what we would've said to him, abt the Factory & his tips for masturbation, what he thought were the best things to say to boys, to bed them in big rooms with balconies, make them stick their tongues out all googly-eyed.

Whiteboys can be horrible, casually cruel, hurt your feelings; white girls plot, set you up, take your life.

If somebody is crying, is it rude to say they're crying over the stupidest shit ever? Even if it is, in fact, the stupidest shit ever?

Don't take this the wrong way, he said. *You look so good, like you do this for money.*

Waiting to meet me after my flight lands, you say *it was easy to spot you, you stand out from the crowd.* What happened to that version of you? Are you not writing me back because you don't want to, or because you have nothing to say?

My mother tells me I should visit more often, take remedial driving lessons.

At salad bars I go for the corn, love seeing those finicky pellets come out when I poop, bright yellow, smelling like nothing.

I like chocolates with gooey mango centers, how I anticipate that sweet viscosity like a boy with his fly open, how the orange spreads & smooths, bowing my head in offering as angry bees fill my throat, his breath against my chest like a crucifix, I break out in hives, the experience entirely feral.

He enjoyed the evening trains, the drunk ones, where everyone was nice, seated comfortably apart, not being too rowdy. He liked how ppl kept their feet off the seats.

You forgot this, he says, arm extended. When I look up, his face rearranges itself into delight, beaming.

关你屁事 NONE OF YOUR BEESWAX

dog's breakfast · my voice a melody
clerihews in here somewhere · my aporia a diet prada

porn name · went to a cbd store, newly opened
will treasure · said *there's a hair in your gummies*

you midland creep show · they examine my moonlit clit
there is only one city · searching for an answer

i like your tongue b/c it's pink · poke my lobster in the nose
you're pinky i'm the brain · share a grilled cheese wit me

john cho · i got kicked out of the pool
don't know · for being too cool for school

dad fell in love wit a hippie · your poems finally
can i call you papi · limewire me a copy

tom daley · don't mean to be bawdy
i think of you daily · but show us that body

i want to be skinny · moving day for stupid sheep
no adult acne · stupid glowstars stupid face

some ppl are worth more than rubies · you want me
rubles not rubies · dismissed wit prejudice

grain de beauté on a ballsack · show me boys in the sticks
my eye socket is obese · show you beez in the trap

PINK STEGOSAURUS

Only a fucked-up poet would write abt boys with thorns. I have many type just like Pokemon. I did college right, found someone 21, voila, free-flowing white sulphur springs & silver mountain water. The brass doesn't hide sun bears from Malaysia, remember that Thai place in Vermont, young Americans inseminating you. Your love letter had footnotes, mad cow disease is a gendered term. Bison backs, seals & walruses, Chocolate Park Tavern for liquor. Totally random lines abt world history, personal history, a favorite myth, a single object, & a song meaningful to you. Last I saw you, we had sushi at Hapa, the one in Cherry Creek, not the one in LoDo (went to that one with my ex). To me you were Bluebeard & the brides, anxious & uneasy, your hands the harshest jury. Tight body lean cuisine—you know your dick is enormous, right. I remember walking around with you after dinner, pounding the pavement like it was our first campaign. I remember us touching, waiting for the light, how it was unseasonably warm, Sleepy's superpredators out & abt. I remember how we put up posters for a boy so obviously lost, posters I now know were of you. It's funny how lives diverge. At my boarding school I protested the prom, opposed plans to hold it at an establishment owned by a parent, an obvious conflict of interest. I nearly got myself expelled. I guess some things don't change. John Lewis calls that good trouble. Good art is always smarter than the person who made it. This poem is very smart, look at the intelligence of this work. I write poems to fight off things I don't want to think abt—pink stegosauruses, body snatchers, & teacups in a storm. Come back, I'll be your 避风塘, love me just a little while. I won't let your words fall to the ground, though shame is an excellent place to hide. I'll leave the light on.

SEAN ★LENNON

"Justice is what love looks like in public, just as tenderness is what love feels like in private"
—Cornel West

He conditions me to like ppl who work odd hours.
He says my legal training gets in the way of our relationship,
says not everything has a neat answer,
says stop picking things apart, searching for a solution,
quit trying to uncover some grand truth.
I try & try & try.

The law is messy, I say,
there *are* rare ppl who act in good faith,
well-intentioned ppl who get it wrong,
but at least the law has *standards*.
I think this is pretty clever but maybe it's a self-own.

The system is monolithic & bureaucratic & I suppose
must be reimagined, refashioned, rising again from ashes.
I imagine everything disintegrating around me, structures &
scaffolding be damned, I am pristine, I will remain standing.

I understand how tenuous existence can be,
when affirmative action can be swept away by the will of the voters,
when your marriage can be invalidated by a majority vote,
when doing what is right & moral can be derided as amnesty.

I know how something can disappear as quickly as it blooms,
how it can be snatched out of your grasp the second you put a name to it.

I think ppl underestimate death, or more specifically, the notion of death,
how it overtakes every facet of your life,
how it is a crushing obsession, an understanding that infects you like the patriarchy,
how it tells you its secrets as you yield to it.

We contain multitudes, you know,
lemon drops & melon balls, sweet & sadistic, turkey & ham.
Is it true that to everything there is a season, I read that somewhere,
that we must think of our lives in seasons,
truer still that we must offer something new every season,
something different, groundbreaking, delightful even, or be eliminated?

He says *I don't like how you come & go,*
this isn't, you know, Denny's or something.
I say you're messy & you meal prep,
you cook for the week & it's creepy.
He says *I'm sorry, I just want you for myself.*
I say how do you predict what you want to eat?

It's abt finding one thing to keep you going,
that's the hack, to keep you fueled up,
discovering it, secreting it away (me), sharing it (whatever).

Lately I have been so delighted by movies abt shoplifters,
& scam artists & ppl really sticking it to the Man,
stealing is bad, of course, but I find myself rooting for the underdog,
revenge of the nerds & some such,
you're programmed in this country to want the underdog to win,
support the team of misfits angling for that championship,
I realize this must be how some ppl feel abt O.J.,
that he slayed justice, that he beat the system.

I remember having a very nice, sit-down kind of breakfast,
at a place called Six Furlong, relatively close to a similar,
more formal establishment named the Gallop, where
the waitstaff went unchanged over decades,
& I was reading an English newspaper & having tea
& being bothered that our breakfast trays were too big,
they clearly didn't fit the table & bumped up against one another,
tipsy virgins jockeying for territory & the scene was comical
yet infuriating & then my porridge was cold.

RULES FOR AMERICAN LIFE

"There's no kindness in your eyes / the way you look at me, it's just not right"—Hilary Duff

"I used to know how to save the world / now I don't know anything anymore"—Justin Chin

:—Once in a blue moon, maybe several times a week,
      I write a truly great American poem;
Here I will tell you abt 8th Street . . .
      my rules for American life—:

Generally: TV always; no sharia law; don't say gay; bathrooms are sacred; no hugging/touching (men); don't pay attention to politics; really, don't, they only need you every 4 years; small talk is an art & national pastime; acceptable small talk topics include complaining abt wife, kids, kids' sports, schedules, Chinese boss; even if you hate sports, you have to pretend; candy corn is the worst; mac-n-cheese is the best side.

When approached by law enforcement: avoid unprovoked flight, do not call them pigs, do not be black, know your rights (you have none), regret your existence, get a lawyer (if still alive).

Things not to do as a person of color: open your eyes, think, walk, drive, shop, talk on cellphone, glance, gaze, smile (unless directed to by a man), laugh, sleep. Oh, & this is very important: don't buy a gun, the Second Amendment is not for us.

There may be limited opportunities for persons of color to feel joy or express happiness. These include: birthdays, church, watching Black Panther, attending sports games (*certain exclusions apply), graduating from community college, winning the lottery (you'll spend it all anyway). Pls note that no open displays of bliss are permitted without prior approval.

In many cases it is acceptable to be Azn (especially Chinese), but you should only speak out for your fellow poc if it is safe to do so (no accent pls); most of the time, stay quiet & low to the ground; never question a White, even if (as is often the case) you are right & they are talking out of their ass; it is preferred that you walk close to edges of rooms & become one with the wall; make sure your flag T-shirt is in heavy use; you know what, plaster flags everywhere; we mean U.S. flags, but you knew that, didn't you, sly dog; when in doubt, play dead. Azns, remember that you are disposable; depending on the matter at hand, you may find yourselves not colored/White enough; you can have opinions but not too many; strive to be mild, not spicy; you are not the arbiter of anything (not even your own food, as a White once told you where to find "the best dumplings"); you are ancillary, don't be threatening. Additionally, Azns are considered highly susceptible to falling in love with Whites; distance from Whites is recommended, horse-blinders are very effective.

All persons of color pls hide your wild & vivacious inner lives; they will steal your ideas & not apologize. They will dilute your thoughts & impressions like the abomination that is 2%. If a White says "let's catch up," they don't wanna see you.

Relatedly, pls learn White-approved celebrity crushes. These include Ryan Gosling, John Mayer, Trump supporter Chris Pratt, Trump supporter & rich child of suburbia Kid Rock, Trump supporter & anal leakage/human pink slime Mario Lopez, Jolie sperm donor Jon Voight, Rick Santorum, Tila Tequila (. . .), that Hot Pockets heiress, Kaia Gerber's right boob, Presley Gerber's face tat, & movie theater hostage Maria Menounos (pls rescue her with your strong ethnic arms).

Now listen—;
I had to cancel someone I met in college
She said something real objectionable
It got on my nerves
I won't bother repeating it
It was offensive
Previously she asked if I got my makeup at the mall,
when I got it at *Neiman Marcus*
She said she didn't like Lohan's new song,
should've ended her then & there
I blocked & deleted her ass after her recent infraction
She should've come correct
Panicked she kept calling me,
first thru apps & then various landlines
I blocked & deleted her from Insta, blocked her on all major platforms
No, she didn't leave any voicemails b/c everyone knows I don't use vm
Anyway she should know that I mercilessly cut ****** off
I'm frightened by how easily I cut a bitch off

(learned that from my ex)
I don't have time for that nonsense
Moche is French for ugly
Just like I don't have time to read your shitty poetry
Let me give you a tip, put some money in your pocket—:
No one cares abt a nothing-war in a country nobody's heard of
The only wars we know are the American ones, thank you very much
(is that 90% of all wars haha)
The only thing we know abt your country are the llamas, boo
We think Fujimori is the world's greatest sushi chef, ok
Don't tell us abt the thousands dead
We're barely concerned with the lives our own state has taken
Jk we don't care
Don't talk abt your bones or surgeries or scar tissue
Your pain is asinine & you don't articulate it very well, anyway
I did not know Mr McCain when I met him
Jk many poets will talk abt Antigone & Sisyphus & the one with the ball of string,
sigh
You tell me you feel bad abt x, y, z
I feel bad you went to Rutgers
That's why they call you the 40-year-old Virgin
You said my centering was inauthentic
Iz okay I like the Pussycat Dolls
You are a yellow cockatiel with orange cheeks
You are lauded for your consumerism
As Hungry-Man says: Eat Like a Man
Which reminds me: I miss Anon Sex Andrew, he likes it raw
So this chick Lea Michele is doing these god-awful ads for HelloFresh
Took a few beats to register who she was
Couldn't remember her real name
Rachel Berry you are a hack
Rachel claims that she works "14-hour days on set" but we all know you not working
gurl
You're only slightly better off than Hayden Panettiere
who, I was surprised to find, is only 30 & no longer working
Dam we weep for her hahaha
What do you say when a bitch claims her favorite movie is Titanic?
FOH: f—k outta here

Some athletes need to shut the fuck up

Novak Djokovic is an anti-vaxxer & a fucking dumbass

Rory McIlroy, to the extent you can understand that accent, says Trump has mishandled the corona

He's just asking to be deported, isn't he?

Yea Trump's keyboard warriors will get him

Personally I agree with fellow ENTP Howard Stern

The people who are voting for Trump . . . he wouldn't even let them in a f—ing hotel. He'd be disgusted by them. Go to Mar-a-Lago, see if there's any people who look like you. I'm talking to you in the audience.

The people Trump despises most love him the most

Trump would be disgusted by the MAGA/KAG crew

The man detests the people who support him but will use & exploit their devotion

This has been true of despots for millennia

Trump recently had to explain to his followers that Madison Avenue meant, as he put it, "(Ad Agencies)"

Do they not have Mad Men in Nebraska?

Speaking of which: Antony Leung, Hong Kong's then-Financial Secretary, bought a Lexus shortly before imposing a new car tax

This dude, a banker worth millions, decided to save a few bucks before resigning in disgrace

Truly shameless

Meanwhile you have U.S. Senators like Richard Burr, Kelly Loeffler, Jim Inhofe, Dianne Feinstein, maybe others (yea name & shame them, that's the tea) capitalizing on privileged information gleaned from confidential briefings

Again, to make a few bucks

Isn't it a maxim that people get the government they deserve?

Evil's power increases, Dostoyevsky observed, proportionately to our disbelief in it

The cronyism, the grifting, the retaliation, the treason—it's all right there

Remember "Individual-1"?

Individual-1 (Trump) orchestrated a felony criminal conspiracy; obstructed justice; retaliated against whistleblowers/witnesses; regularly used mob language like "rat"; got impeached for abuse of power; & has seen his top officials & personal lawyer become felons

But sure the *Obama* administration is the scandalous one

Yea ok thx

(I will, however, note that human hemorrhoid Jim Clapper turned perjury into an art form, war criminal John Brennan was a waterboarding/extrajudicial killing prick, &

Obama made horrible personnel choices like putting in Jim Comey & hand-picking widely-reviled DNC chair & Hamilton fanatic Debbie Wasserman Schultz. & how could we forget the mass deportations, Operation Fast-n-Furious, Valerie Jarrett, & Saint Michelle's petty feud with Desirée Rogers?)

—in any case, all ****** ***** does is write abt mass shootings & police brutality & not in an interesting way, some good poems but his perspectives are cliche*

I don't think he offers anything fresh, he actually used the phrase "now more than ever" in an interview, can you believe that shit

Ultimately he writes from a position of weakness . . .

*This is a work of fiction. Names, characters, events & incidents are products of the author's imagination. Any resemblance to actual persons or events is purely coincidental. Names have been obscured to protect the guilty.

  Define my poetry? *Caution: Extreme Cuteness*

(—I recommend reading it . . . it's visually arresting, a sensual buffet, bacchanal

Thank you for playing, despite the odds

Wear cologne to bed, you never know who'll be visiting

I laughed so hard when your boyfriend took your thumb

  & unlocked your phone

I cried so hard when your boyfriend took your face

  & emptied your acct

When I tell you abt my manuscript

  why you gotta assume iz titled \<Dreams of Goddess Napalm\>

  or \<Chicken in Hoisin Sauce\>

Have you heard the axiom that one American life is worth more than 100 foreign ones?

  Maybe if you weigh us haha obesity

Having said that: notice that animal cruelty is still more swiftly prosecuted than crimes against certain humans & by this I mean blacks

  Persons of color still waiting for justice

but you know what they say abt Lady Justice:

  overly emotional, very slutty, takes forever to get ready ha

The Golden Rule of America is that you'll never be enough—;

  . . . *i.e.,* straight enough, light-skinned enough, masculine enough, athletic enough, funny enough, pure enough, rich enough . . . so why not have fun & fuck shit up while you're at it

记得我们有约 • 不见不散

/ / /

AMERICA'S SWEETHEART

is Brett a human boy with sneakers and a best friend named Tate or Donovan or Tate Donovan and a cat named PJ who thinks self-driving cars are the future who is into sports but doesn't talk about it incessantly and watches porn but nothing too kinky Brett in Poli Sci class who skips an exam to go to Hersheypark where he inevitably has his hand up the skirt of some unsuspecting girl who thinks she has found the one and perfect to bring home to her family in Swarthmore and hair like J.Crew model circa 2008 and like the chick in Umbrella Academy who can make people do things Brett knows he's cute with an unassuming floppy brown mop that could easily be a fashion haircut that is conservative yet modern and slick and clean and costs more than John Edwards' or AOC's and could independently take over a motel in Iowa Young Brett with his birthright citizenship and Fourteenth Amendment protections he never really needs and always treats other people with respect and never accidentally replies-all with something indecent or inappropriate so PC principal never has to say shit Brett who orders a Tito's and soda though the restaurant doesn't serve hard liquor and yet the mousy waitress scrambles to go someplace sketchy on Sixth Avenue to get it so Brett is happy though he never throws a tantrum in public but she doesn't know that Brett is an undecided voter

MOOSE KNUCKLES

You have your speed-dial pussies, pregnant as possum
Split second, black palms, an instant

Aren't you trying to support me, husband me up
So I can be a trophy

I am my own trophy
& didn't yo mama say that *need* & *want* are different things?

Nikki says most rabbis Jewish
You claim to hate it here but I don't like it anywhere

I call you Adam, take your light-skinned
white-passing bush leagues

your gratuitous apple-bobbing
insane clown posse

your pale here's-a-suggestion narcissism
sweet meaning screwed up

breath spooky on my earlobes
tongue swimming between my cheeks

your howling cosmology
pug nose closer than it appears

Your second & third waves
Mr Postman's dick hanging out his shorts

Whiteboys in puffer coats, arm in arm
Blond, cream-smooth legs ready to break some hearts

Down to keep me out like the cold
Their eyes wander, accents blur, hard to place

I could use a little fortune in my cookie
[raucous laughter, aggressively virile]

When Reagan was President
P.Y.T. meant pretty young thing

Why doesn't Tyehimba Jess write a book
called *Infinite Jess?*

Now, Chelsea Clinton squinting, this glow really slaps
The je ne sais quoi, these notes on fear

The one who made it out /// the one who got away
(Same one?)

A big rabbit, actually a horse
How the hell did we learn to care for small animals?

Light me up monstrous & milky
Anything is possible here in the cosmos

The moon icing over
Your rimless dark, ever-present & empty

The trick to gardening is ample patience
& an elaborate staff

~

HAIBUN FOR GIA

Why are you hungry, Gia Carangi? Have you ever been so obsessed with someone that you can't sleep? Were you devastated when you realized that they were a sentient being with their own selfish needs & wants? How did you get your eyebrows so bushy? Do you know the difference between broken-heartedness & dejection? Do you know that a broken heart brings us closer to the service of God, but dejection corrodes service? Why do you keep touching your elbows like that? How much do you love the part in Snatched where Randall Park's character is breaking up with Amy Schumer's & he says his band is blowing up & where he's going there's gonna be a ton of pussy but she mishears & thinks he says inspiration & finally she hears pussy? Have you ever written a love letter to someone you've never met? Did you remember to get groceries that last the week? Has a boy ever made you levitate? How do you feel abt winged monkeys? Have you ever been to Flushing, Queens? What do you think when a singer gets on one of those scoring karaoke machines & only gets 50/100 on their own song or when a famous person takes a "which famous person are you?" quiz & doesn't get themselves as a result? How do you feel abt lambs bleating & the wonder & hurt of being & the wet delight of a tongue & being America's prom queen & kicking off your Manolos & pure unadulterated terror? Is it too much to ask for a nice fucking house & good fucking friends? Do you like to test ppl? What do you want ppl to say abt you when you die? Or do you not care? How do you feel abt remote learning? Do you need a blanket?

*

Your yukata falls open, summer weight,
not blossoms but cherries

Bare feet wincing, you slide open the shoji

Shivering

A PARTY OF ANIMALS

"If you want to win, you gotta learn how to play head games"—Foreigner

"One must be a fox to recognize traps, and a lion to frighten wolves"—Machiavelli

*

Gideon liked John's office job since every day at certain hours he knew exactly where John would be.

He was more and more convinced that John's easy demeanor wasn't an act.

He liked John's gentle ribbing, his subtle teasing, his recovering-frat-boy vibes, his potential problem with drink.

He liked John's little jokes, the ones that made political points but didn't hit you in the face with them.

He liked John's patience, his attentiveness, though he supposed that was part of his job.

You know who has it worst? John asked once. An appropriate pause followed. *Male models*, he declared dramatically. *Chronically underpaid, one of the few areas where men are paid less than women, generally regarded as being dumb as rocks and pretty vessels with no souls. And that is why I left the world of male modeling.* He said this deadpan, with a twinkle in his eye.

Gideon laughed but in the moment was more focused on John's face. Greek or Roman beauty, an American sensibility, features etched intaglio. A modern day Antinous, brown hair shiny, lips thick and glossy. Gideon admired John's strong legs, wanted to touch his tanline, his delicate ankles. He thought about how, if given the opportunity, he would undo John's belt buckle, fingers quick as a thief's, slip off his boxers, and get to work. He would show John a good time.

Gideon had looked it up. The New York Rules of Professional Conduct, effective April 1, 2009, and with commentary as amended through June 1, 2018, provides that a lawyer shall not:

employ coercion, intimidation or undue influence in entering into sexual relations incident to any professional representation by the lawyer or the lawyer's firm . . .

Gideon was turned on by the idea that his fantasy was something accounted for in the rules of professional responsibility, the same strictures John was bound by. What Gideon wanted to do to John was a profanation, unspeakable and erotic. For John, Gideon felt a desire trembling on the edge of hostility, how he teetered with want, to hold John and see his eyes bistered by desire, consumed by confusion. Gideon would be the song John listened to when he fucked his high-school girlfriend, remastered. He imagined John's yellow Mustang, Cruel Summer playing in the background, how his girlfriend couldn't handle his size or stamina.

With John around, Gideon lived always in the fire of his own smoldering combustion, perishing and born again at every instant. He entered over and over again into that cauldron of sex, flesh, blood, bone, and marrow. Each time he emerged unscathed like a lizard that shed its tail, right in the nick of time. One night Gideon dreamt that John had written him. But of course he hadn't. Gideon masturbated not 5 minutes after waking up, a record for him, moaning so loudly he had awoken his roommate.

Gideon thought about how John looked fat and young in the right places. John was older, of course, but not that much older where it got weird. In the shower Gideon would pretend that his hands were John's, touching himself, soaping every inch of his skin like a studious pastry chef, mouthing the things he wouldn't say to John, attorney-client privilege notwithstanding.

He wanted to feel John's nails digging into him, pressing shell-pink welts into his pale skin, raising little bruises to the surface. John would coax his body into submission, talk him into having a body at all, one to excavate, to inquire deeply about, Gideon the prettiest star, the actor in a leading role. John would do that thing with his mouth, his long teeth clicking, meeting no resistance like a blade to leather, his nerve-endings tingling like a bright memory, first prize at the science fair. He would embrace the wonder and hurt and delight and surge, an elaborate mating ritual, some exotic dance, a party of animals over as suddenly as it began. He wanted John to leave him shaking like a polaroid picture.

John made Gideon want to scream, raise hell, play dress up in his lawyerly clothes, fresh from the drycleaners, plastic sheath still crinkling. He thought about what he'd wear for his deposition, spent more time figuring that out than going over the testimony in his mind. He wondered what people would say if they knew he had a crush on his lawyer.

He imagined John coming home to him after work. He would kick off his shoes, sit on the edge of the bed, undress in stages, ask about Gideon's day, ruffle Gideon's hair, put his nose to Gideon's head and take a big whiff. They would kiss gently at first, then passionately, maybe oral if John wasn't too tired. Feeling beautifully spent, Gideon would heat up some meatloaf, fixed extra mustardy the way John liked it, and they would settle into their nightly routine of strong drinks and 80s movies.

Are you okay, John asked. *Lost you for a second there*. Gideon blinked. You would never lose me, Gideon thought. You have me. You have me.

ELECTRIC LEMON

You know the story
He became the rain
Then a roaring fire
Face impassive
Flames licking warm & thick & ferocious
The furl of his shirt in hot air
The room glowed
The walls cracked & fissured
The ceiling deposited poisonous fruit
It was a forest & then it wasn't
She watched the boy disappear into a man
& the man disappear into a desert
When the basement started filling with foxes
They vowed never to play house again

DISPATCHES FROM SUPPER CLUB

"The edge of a lie I offered you / the smell of your body behind a flannel shirt"—Douglas Crase

"The shirt seemed heavy until he saw there was another shirt inside it . . . the pair like two skins, one inside the other, two in one"—Annie Proulx

show yourself
  revelatory goodness
  wrapped tighter & tighter ..

give me shelter
  cruelty dressed as kindness
  glory to be the thing tucked discreetly in your dinner jacket ..

photo of 5 or 6 dartmouth boys admittedly v cute
  caption paul ryan intern photo
  pheromones & ropes ..

your intermittent service
  indiscretions seeped in clay
  your peony - my mouth ..

boys on skateboards
  crushed in foil
  my heart in hiding ..

little lamb & sleeping bear
  roe v wade whiplash
  secrets to divulge ..

if i could
  i would forget your
  dispatches from supper club ..

LITTLE DOM'S PLEASURE CAMP

"Bodies have always wanted only one thing, to be aimless"—Wayne Koestenbaum

照妖镜 :: *in Chinese lore, mirrors with mysterious properties can reveal & control demons. These magic mirrors reflect a demon's true form.*

Strut like Pat Cleveland / no idea who the fuck you are / leave yams of perpetual knowledge / you can scurry away now / hot showers make me happy / skinny legs make me horny / if the Marlboro Man was paid in cigarettes / was he ever really paid / hordes of models in NYC with expensive clothes / & no rent money / want your hand in the small of my back / your eyes looking down, anticipating / revenge beers in the Yeti cooler / stupid boys & their videogames / talk wit ur hips, my heavenly position / macan is Indonesian for tiger / makan is Indonesian for eat / there is a Midtown restaurant only selling unagi / & I think about what a luxury that is / remember *things* / remember *living* / wish I understood the Renaissance the way I understand my ejaculate / I am proudest of my poetry, thank you for your concurrence / kiss my Chinese finger trap yea / embrace my Chinese water torture yea / I like coming-of-age quest flicks like Superbad b/c aren't we all just trying to get to the party / I want silver Porsche but you're silver Pontiac, / Gary Oldman but you're Gary Busey / Kim Basinger made me a caprese sandwich, / Michelle Pfeiffer made me butternut squash soup that tasted better than it looked / Kasabian is a cool band name / Dane DeHaan was my pity fuck / I think about the highest floor on the Bowery, / coasting down the West Side Highway, / nearly killing that dude / do I look relaxed like edamame dumplings in broth / I'm the best motivational speaker you'll ever meet / you cornteen South of France / ice cream sandwiches & Robitussin chasin' / coochie we always go into it blindly / Neiman Marcus filed for Chapter 11 / AMC has $4.85 billion in long-term debt / are billiard ball colors & numbers standardized / don't ask me to send you a list of restaurant recommendations when you're not going to a single one you fucking bitch reverend / at Apple & Amazon, employees pay for their food; Facebook & Google, company pays / we are gym class heroes / fatboy & lazyman / I'm needy & high maintenance but your [sic] ugly / some writing advice for you (I take Venmo) / shorter sentences, cut cut cut, simplify, don't explain, don't try to impress, I'm smarter than you, surprise, use uncommon pairings & phrasing / the banana bread of life / the Harvard of community colleges / the face of a boy who loves you / Florida: Evan & beaches, though Evan likes Chicago better / pool boy in gingham shorts, tall & cool

& full of gin / I'm the kind to shave my legs in the dark / you said that Hegel was an Austrian tennis player / hooked on battlefields & conjugal visits / maybe bologna / nostalgic for Evan, crayons, & Barneys New York / sentimentality shaking the nation from its sleep / the impeachable former Arkansas governor / every great story is two things: totally familiar, yet absolutely foreign / this poem is over / well, that was some weird shit •

RUSH, RUSH

Calling all armchair/
Monday morning quarterbacks
Backseat drivers
Couch potatoes
Warriors/lovers of the weekend
Why are y'all reviled?
I want someone beautiful & terrifying,
self-destructive tendencies but no cavities
Unchallenged, nay, unmolested by the law,
kind enough to offer his fleece,
fix me dinner, join the protest
Really into manual labor,
manicured hands/feet from a magazine
Superb ass, adored by shorts,
slippery tongue breaking curfew
I want someone indulging my skin,
wondering *why haven't I tasted this before?*
Don't let me get side-tracked y'all
This is a poem abt blowjobs

BLACK & WHITE

"You could not be born at a better period than the present, when we have lost everything"
—Simone Weil

When a white womxn smile
I remember the first time
you forgot my birthday
When a blk womxn ax *do you know what poetry snaps are*
I resolved to become a great, nay, legendary poet
\ Tell me, dear reader, how am I doing?
Please consider this application for asylum
couriered to Angela Merkel
Madam for financiers
phone ringing off the hook
You can be my original sin
玉石俱焚
obliterating jade & stone, destroying indiscriminately
Weird when big dudes bottom
iz like putting toothpaste back in the tube
I don't know how to love something so big
\ This is not a sexual reference
Like when I told W— that hugging him felt like holding the world
\ or was it the universe
Or when I told J— that I wanted that feeling to be permanent
\ like a gravestone
Or when I told K— that he should leave his girlfriend
\ so tall but powerless & drowning in his own indecision
\ & in that avalanche of emotion I could've ended him with my heat vision
Or the other K— who held my hand & led me around the park
\ cute feet in sneakers blinding white
\ how I said *what does this make us* & he didn't answer
Or R— when he told me he was moving to San Francisco to be an artist
\ & we touched & touched & touched & touched
\ until glitter rained down on us like righteousness
曾经沧海难为水 • 除却巫山不是云
\ if you've seen the ocean, what's a small stream

\ if you've been in a rainstorm, what's a light drizzle
\ been there, done that, but
Bless the boys who don't know any better
If only their resolve were hard
like the tree that wouldn't bend
& the bottle
that wouldn't break

WITHOUT FEAR OR FAVOR

if america is an experiment, we're the guinea pigs
article 51-a (g) of the indian constitution provides:
"it shall be the duty of every citizen * * * to have compassion for living creatures"
want your kiss & baby back ribs
dance mirror & woe
gorge on redheads & birthday cake
we board the lifeboats in this order: no cops, ever
deflated life rafts & peaceful tear gas
forget your white allyship
the first thing we do: kill all the lawyers
backyards covered in soot
i'm the mozart of trolling
& the beethoven of dissing
the greco-roman crocodile chose you
ebony & ivory
in that moment i knew neglect
like when zach galifianakis ax brie larson:
"you won best actress—have you ever thought of aiming higher and trying to win
best actor?"
r u dan quayle cuz u can be my potato——e
无依无靠
no one to rely on
boy gulps
you smell me
whip your head round
i catch your eye
you're mad fit
slide off those shorts
moo for me
daz queer theory

UGLYCUTE

"I love you too / don't fuck up my hair / I can't believe you almost fisted me today"
—Eileen Myles

In China, "bitten peach" is code for queerness. There was once a handsome courtier named Xia Mizi who halved a juicy peach so his lover, Duke Ling of Wei, could taste it as well. Of coz, every time a Chinese has something good, a White has to snatch it—fuck it—cum in it. The phrase "cut sleeve" also refers to queerness. Emperor Ai, who ruled during the Han Dynasty, shared a bed with his lover Dong Xian. After a nap, the Emperor cut off his own sleeve to avoid disturbing his sleeping lover.

Seeing him suave in his weathered, waxy jacket, bellows pockets sized for snacks, stubs, & receipts, you want to know if he's ever written abt you. You say *take me on your travels, I'm sure the Nepalese have something to teach me.* I'm going to Patagonia, he replies, worn satchel in hand, well-traveled weekend bag at his desert-booted feet. *Ppl hate Amtrak's new meals so much . . . 125 pages of complaints the first year,* you whine, but his back is already turned, you hare-brained Tom, Dick, & Harry. *I'll drown myself in the Bosphorus,* you insist.

Mm, fathers should neither be seen nor heard. Ghost fathers, substitute daddies, & Holy Grail Zaddies: cocks destroyed, burned off, botched like a Picasso. Don't compare yourself to me, ever, I wish gaping wounds, mono, & pink eye on you. Check your lipstick b4 you come talk to me. There's no room for disagreement in my life, we will activate Bill Barr & activate him strongly. Dancemonkey selfie, dancemonkey says wut? A lawyer who represent hisself has a fool for a client.

The thing abt me is I don't say shit I don't mean. Capisce? Once I outran a show-offy dolphin. At least I thought I did. Thank you, have a good life.

SWEET TORTURE

I order my life around the red-crowned crane,
yes, that dignified bird of sweet immortality,
lacquered votive offering to myself.
The way you take in my Mutual of Omaha,
sex with you is like laying with a dragon.
I know you can kill me with your bare hands,
filthy & fearsome.
Tame your savage breath,
draw from me, these Lazarus Pits
an erotic terror.
Yeah, well,
you can't keep or hold a man's attention.
Let me introduce you to New York's true finest,
you should know that I can slay you in a second.
All is for naught the second you open your mouth,
your lumbering burden rendered nothing,
goat sacrifice in a seersucker suit.
Like Zhang Ziyi in Rush Hour 2,
I'll bleed you out Santería style,
yes, that rug really tied the room together.
You're normal like a Macy's polo shirt,
scratchy cotton hugging your nipples the wrong way,
you know, that's your opinion,
man.

TWO SHAKES OF A LAMB'S TAIL

i send my assembly-line boy back:

reset his factory settings, my hands remember how he likes it

wipe his rosy cheeks, flick his pink nipples one last time

commit his little moans to memory, his blue eyes glowing with promise

take his box out of storage, a hasbro grave,

geoffrey's gone like god & good fortune

admire his bulging cow eyes & long lean legs, achingly beautiful smoothness

straighten his white shirt, lower him into the abyss

lay packing peanuts on him (there's a penis joke here),

make sure the plastic isn't suffocating

i'll miss him, i'm sure, but

doesn't it just eat at you when a boy is too perfect?

INCENDIARY CHXNXMXN

XN XNGLXSH-CHXNXSX PHRXSXBXXK (1875)

X CXMPLXTX LXST XF WXLLS, FXRGX & CX'S
CXLXFXRNXX, NXVXDX, XTC.

CXMPXLXD BY WXNG SXM XND XSSXSTXNTS

* * *

WHXT GXXDS HXVX YXX FXR SXLX?

I HXVX XLL KXNDS

I WXNT TX GXT X PXXR XF YXXR BXST PXNTS

WHXT DX YXX XSK FXR THXM?

&   CXN YXX TXKX LXSS FXR THXM?

X CXNNXT, SXR

WXLL YXX SXLL XN CRXDXT?

XNLY CXSH, SXR

WX PXY VXRY HXXVY DXTY XN XXR BXST GXXDS

SXMX MXN LXSX CXPXTXL

&   SXMX MXN GXT PRXFXTS

BXY XS MXNY XS YXX LXKX

CXN YXX LXT MX SXX XT?

YXXR CXCK, X MXXN

SPOONING IS STUPID

⏑　　　⏑

Let's get down to brass tacks
If you love this country, you wake up every day in
fucking awe
It fucking takes your breath away
Yet, as it turns out, we've been lied to
"Prickly pears" are achilly cacti
"Peanut butter" contains neither nuts nor butter

        Thin cigarette between your teeth
        You pat me on the back
        Tell me abt your demons, your body
        Lord set aside that nagging truth
        Tell it slant like my eyes
        Ash on your tongue, Mount Nittany looms like death & taxes

        Yeats said *out of the quarrel with others we make rhetoric*
        out of the quarrel with ourselves we make poetry
        Tupac said *the blacker the berry, the sweeter the juice*
        the darker the flesh, the deeper the roots
        My voice catches when I say—: *if the British cared abt us*
        they would've granted us citizenship

50% of Roger Federer's name is *er*
Snickers have a dick vein
Will Ferrell is the sexy hunk of a Catholic high school
Not as funny as the original, but Justin Bieber dies
Winner winner chicken dinner
[人生百态] I'm a hunter, a hare
Original fruit medley
Not you, not you
        Two truths & a lie—: *"I guard my life with no apologies.*
        My concerns are small and personal."—Essex Hemphill

"Asia is rising against me.
I haven't got a chinaman's chance." —Allen Ginsberg

I push the men's room door,
smiling as they say—: *wrong one*

STOP TRYING TO MAKE FETCH HAPPEN

Stop trying to make food sexy
Food is inherently sexy
I'm sitting in the vegan section of my favorite haunt,
a chicken joint called *The Only Pollo That Matters*
If you get this brilliant & layered joke we can be friends
I know I have a problem when Dim Andrew says I'm Mayor of the place
Whiteness confers greatness
I wonder: *is it a strong mayor-weak council form of government?*
Do I have control over the public schools? *Who appoints the police chief?* Fuck the police
Dim Andrew makes me want to get off to his favorite porno, even if it's not my style
I think Dim Andrew likes interracial—in adult video,
interracial means white mxn & black womxn (& never the other way round)
I don't remember why, but I want what's his
He follows me home & we watch the Discovery Channel
What do you even say to someone who's 19? *Can I make you a snack?*
I don't want to be "in conversation with" anyone—my best dinner guests are dead
I hate Kenneth Koch, str8 & easily the worst of the lot
Frenzied & horny, Dim Andrew says *how long have you been a queen?*
He's my blond furniture & I fancy myself a critic with a good eye
He imagines himself a good-girl-gone-bad, aura of neediness & toxicity
Paranoid & untidy, he's an empire to be coddled
Avatar of sex, thin skin of a leviathan
Have you ever noticed that our bald eagle is so different from the Germans'?
Theirs is black with a red beak, red tongue, & red feet on a golden backdrop
Empires are obsessed with eagles, which symbolize power & dominion
There are double-headed eagles and the Russians even like triple-headed eagles, kind
of gross
For some reason my mind keeps going back to the Desert Eagle
Dim Andrew says *that's gun culture for you*
He who thought Cheech & Chong were the conjoined twins reaches over
Mmmm dominate me daddy shield me daddy comport me daddy consummate me
daddy siphon me daddy surprise me daddy impersonate me daddy incapacitate me
daddy subrogate me daddy scaffold me daddy compartmentalize me daddy
dispossess me daddy get off me daddy . . . time for the beautiful revenge of self-love,
Okay . . . now you go—
Bonne chance—

RAGE IS JUST A NUMBER

I call home but it's not there. I push
Brendan's mouth open with my
tongue, his neck so inviting.

He lets me touch him till he shudders.
I've learned to feed the ducks within
me. They're always hungry.

I'm the bag of old crusts, a vessel for
your hate: flip me over, turn me inside
out.

You can journal your disappointment
later.

CHILDREN OF THE REVOLUTION

raid my closet   yea rate it too   yea 10s across the board
raid my pantry   yea peanut butter crackers   sticky sticky steamy polenta
indian summer unseasonably warm   the fabled mama grizzlies
        rawr rawr rawr devour   nick jonas diabetic sperm   cutest of the jonai
body slick   dog-tired   face a perfect o   . .   o king of prussia
my flat pancake azn face has you hungry   get on top repugnance   open up teacup
crawling up your white thighs & outstretched palms   rip me apart pulled pork
lie on me sizzling lamb chop   everything is costume   salt & pepper rib
squeeze me criss angel mindfreak   fade into your musculature carl phillips
kiss me calamari briny salty sweet chili sauce   make me hear faint sirens of you
singing off-key but it feels so good   magical choreography monkey abu
we'll be quiet night sky   hamster that bit me when i was 6   you have been warned
i've been plotting my revenge ever since   i remember this   summertime sadness
checkerboard vans   tall geeks with confidence issues   mercury rising black ****** moa
        bloom like orlando   futuresex lovesongs
on the apps i was wondering why everyone was a registered nurse   turns out RN
means RIGHT NOW   more activity than a drive-thru on thursday night
i measure my worth by how quickly you change your settings to
        DELETE CHATS . . 24 HOURS AFTER VIEWING rather than immediately after viewing
good boy open wide   open your throat terrible beauty   earthiness & passion
body & struggle & suet   lion heart nature of things   spilling blood & havoc
line some quarters up on your dick   priest of ruin   ram his eye till glitter comes out
        pay for lunch washing dishes   they better have free refills up in here
coming in you ask if i'm decent
                                hunny
        i'm *exceptional*

        •

CHILDHOOD IDOLS

"We wanted them to wander over,
place deep wet underarms to
our lips, and then their white
asses, then those loud mouths?"
—Dennis Cooper

"Oh no, you don't understand, this is an Alaïa!"
—Cher Horowitz

— — —

Pale boy juicy rubies : nerves frayed black-winged birds
taste of copper : strange & lovely to touch : needing a
sweet escape : i opt in : flesh scraping fear do do do
suzanne vega : make & model of his lips : classic mustang
turning into my own turning until i react : whistling the
star-spangled banner into my throat : small breath small
breath touch mouth my neck : stay of execution too late :
modesty flat white like coffee : bacon butty a fine kiss :
soaked in acqua di gio : or is it dior sauvage : sean o'pry on
a white horse : le cuir trouve la lame : piercing the veil of
insecurity : you come upon me : cooing : u ask what does
that mean : i ask why must words have meaning : mc
confidential : sticky fingers & two pints : les sucettes :
laisse tomber les filles : ne dis rien : comment te dire adieu?
: dis-lui que je l'aime : je suis venu te dire que je m'en vais :
souviens-toi de m'oublier : figure this shit out yourself :
indomitable spirit : fiance fled to keep her sanity : you
basic ass : **judy chicago is dead** : dax exclamation with no
point : nick cave & the bad seeds : u step out madiba vibes
: pockets of tenderness : lick like ur life depends on it : my
signature is boss : my signature is wealthy : my signature
is legendary : loopy loop : strong & decisive : elegant &
evocative : mild-mannered yet firm : dressed to impress :
mother monster sings *RedOne* : but b/c of the autotune : i

think she's saying red wine : so nice of her to sing about
wine : berries turn my tongue darkly : stained like an iraqi
finger : we are liberators : how's that going? : well they
have the simpsons now & they didn't have it before : so
there : you fill me with unclean secrets : pour dirty change
into my jar : tell me no double-dipping : marathon kisses
out of fairy tales : bodies shining : elusive & swooning :
elaborate dance rehearsed but sloppy : veins in marble :
patina of the mind : surfaces laid with tarp : devout
astroturf : high school nights recalling high school days : in
my head you're danny phantom : jeremy : make me : spin :
gentle soul : cloud to touch : full mouth smirking : thin lip
& muscle : long teeth : my neck : stars laid deep in ur
dreams : skittish fawn soft : morning light jewel tones &
baubles : sun-kissed & seizing : diffidence knitting ur
brows : did they teach you that in toms river : two oceans
jealous of summer : seaweed clusters tossed in black : ink
pours from rock : scrape our feet on shells : motherfucker
gentleman : when estelle sings *you can be my American boy,*
American boy : i know exactly what she's saying : the feels
swelling inside me : trying to forget she's singing about
kanye west : white house blue accents : can't hear anything
but blue & white blue & white blue & white : nittany lions
: was ur middle name reid : or hart : would we like
ourselves : fighting fish sarah barracuda : oxblood trail : splintered
tesserae : red cliff angst : NSA means no strings
attached : rebel rebel : wild unraveling : scarlet & thistle &
still : blush & seed : barbra streisand : series regular on
Cops : so yves klein : bleu steak : tartare & fries : blue
suede blue loafers blue socks electric blue crashing white
piping jeremy dafour : haribo smurfs red white & blue 2.49
$: you can't hurt me now shark : i've plied you with
absinthe & purple shimmer : princely gates & silkscreen
thrushes : zipped in turquoise & cyan : opal twisting
through them : carla bruni freak in the sheets : flick flick
feet frank sinatra : tiny tiny dots damien hirst : moths
moths butterflies lee mcqueen : bonfire orchards dried &
hung : local patches of c*ck : ashes fall fendi coat : apollo's

belt gut love : happiness is a warm gun : tucked under my arm : you look best when you're not breathing : chilling poison ivy gaze empty : famous last words : *are you a serial killer?* : truth is the wildest thing : d i s t u r b i a : vinyl playing pumped-up kicks wall-to-wall shag carpet : holster packin : safe in ur mouth : pivotal moment of my life : smothering sex : shifting urself again & again : lean of ur chest rising & falling : threat of bruise on ur lip : tight of my grip : arm pinned over ur head : te ves muerto •

THE MALE OF THE SPECIES

"Now faith is confidence in what we hope for and assurance about what we do not see"
—Hebrews 11:1

Fulfill my week, streaked pippin, Pennsylvania butter sweet
Daddy was a mall cop, Mama was a mongoose
The effect of beauty on the mind, absolute shit
Cook for your macho, do the salty dance

Porn name Martin Garrish, nerves of steel
Slip in & out of mild depression, stoop to enter Benedict Canyon
Armored exterior Chinese wanna eat me
Steely demeanor Anna wanna meet me

Porn name Cathy Park Hung, hot felon, armed career criminal
Die for vain freedoms over a Solo cup
Give your mouth a test drive
Work you long division, binge you new season
Spread your fresh butter, kind of manspreading you like
Swap spit, *passim*, there it is
Scratch your back, rub my lobster's belly
Flay my kill, call it my cursed child
Baby look at these hands
I have mastered love

Check you out Ezra Pound
Tenn Williams called his drug tablets "pinkies"
& sexual conquests "nightingales"
Are you dead?
Feelings snag on nipple ring
Treat you like a snack when you're a full meal
That was obviously dicta

I'm perfectly lucid
fumbling for my key to the city
Tribeca after dark
Blackened cauliflower & tahini

My conditional Azn belonging
(Everyone else has to hyphenate.)
Your white & hetero wedding cake topper
Take turns trying on each other's skin
(Hot pan, skin-side down, don't touch, get the crispiest skin.)
(Get up.) (Eat again.)

REQUIEM FOR TOOTHY TILE & GREY GOOSE

After Ted Casablanca

"Like two white people kissing in the rain & it is always / white people kissing in the rain on television & it is a question / of hair, I imagine"—Hanif Abdurraqib

"With cotton candy armpits and sugary / crevices, sweat glazing your donut skin / have you ever been fat, Brad?"—Aaron Smith

•

Hey Upper East Siders,

Once there was an up-&-coming star ("Toothy Tile") whose princess birthday cake was made famous by Amy Schumer; many years after the fact, he praised his dearly departed co-star for refusing to tell a homophobic joke at the Oscars.

Once there was a young actor who came to fame in a highly-regarded film about queer love; he "dated" the celebrity offspring of an American A-lister (once a darling, now a trainwreck) & a foreign singer.

Once there was an actor who came up through the Disney ranks & later dramatically transformed his body for a role in which he wore red shorts; his address was 5601 Briarcliff Road.

Once there was a celebrity couple (with showbiz offspring) in a prominent lavender marriage; the man used to be A-list but has had several recent flops, the woman is B-list & mostly TV.

Once there was a tween heartthrob in a family enterprise who married a foreign, B-list mostly movie actress who saw moderate success with a patriotic TV series.

Once there was a Disney alumnus who married a foreign actress known mostly for a bit role on pay TV & modelling for Louis Vuitton; he was linked to an Azn-American fashion designer.

Once there was an all-American model-turned-actor (think Abercrombie) who married then split with a celebrity florist after many years in the glass closet.

Once there was a foreign dual-threat actor all of you know from a longstanding comic book franchise who married an actress friend in a lavender marriage; he has a great singing voice.

Once there was a foreign actor who played an icon in a biopic & also saw success in a role adjacent to a world-famous (also foreign) children's book franchise; he is in a lavender marriage that will end soon.

Once there was an A-list bona fide movie star who came to fame in a film about a ship; he recently appeared in a throwback flick directed by the misogynistic A-list director who hates Bruce Lee.

Once there was a permanent A-list movie star who played an iconic character named after a body of water; he married a foreign professional & maimed an underaged love interest in a foreign country.

Once there was a B (maybe C) list mostly TV actor who was noticeably passed over for a big-screen role; his career has seen a resurgence since his replacement was filmed choking a fan in a Nordic country.

Once there was a foreign actor known for his twinkishness & crying when his role in a lucrative franchise was threatened by external events; he is Toothy Tile's latest flame.

Once there was an A-list movie star who came to prominence in a frat-favorite film set in Vegas; he "dated" & later had a child with a known foreign beard.

Once there was a straw-haired, budding foreign actor who "dated" an A-list American singer known for her Girl Next Door image & stable of closeted "boyfriends."

Once there was a foreign singer who was perhaps the first or second most popular in his group; his recent solo outing was praised by an A-list singer who once sang about white-winged doves.

Once there was a boybander-turned-solo-act who was perhaps the third or fourth most popular in his group; he shares a name with a famous river.

Once there was a buff heartthrob who came to fame in a tween franchise but has since only appeared in box-office bombs; he once dated the closeted offspring of a permanent A-list action-hero-turned-politician.

Once there was a tween idol who is not the most famous member of his family & later came out as bisexual; he is on serious drugs & has resorted to sleeping with older men for money.

Once there was a boy, a boy with perfect imperfections, a boy who knew all the words,

& he loved them all.

垃圾 GARBAGE

This is how we start the decade: with ample confidence,
stiff as a Drum Major,
I avoid you so you can't avoid me
Mom talks abt eating bugs, pulling their legs off & swallowing them whole
Fuck, Avedon makes me look really svelte
They can't keep their paws off me
Rarified taste buds & elite nose
Celebrate your illicit spoils
Save your dollar-store morals
I write a poem abt Cody Fern,
make hasty fuck Luc Defont
Earthly courtesans with otherworldly mouths,
ghost hands on my body,
Bust in my mouth, Tide Pod clean & creamy
The rest of you please go—
take your gross hands & syphilis breath with you,
rush off a cliff like a herd of swine, drown yourselves, there's no excuse
Your book is horrible, it's turkey jizz
You tout your alphabet of mo(u)rning & parade your grammar of grief
Let me recite the ABCs of desire & sketch a geometry of adorations,
I'll show you how the real tuck is done
I prefer the ones who weren't captured, the ones who ask for things
I send him a note & he doesn't reply
He can die, I don't wanna be untouched broccoli
I hate his sex, his mind over matter
I watch your legs dangle still in the water, handsome & carefree
You are my instrumentality, barefoot with a bottle of wine
Freshly aglimmer your meat ragu, that hamburger helper
Lather me in rigatoni chicken & pesto, I know plenty that you don't—
sausage & pepperoni a possibility
Make up a lil song to remember the number to Frank's Pizza
Gimme that Boyardee kiss, so deep, such wow
Muah—make sure the witness tells the truth
How's my English now?

ROSEBUD

Ukase :: You like it
You give it

COWBOYS ARE MY WEAKNESS

A boy, to put it plainly, is a loathsome thing

Drifted into this life
The only koan I know is Andy
O aborted picnic at Storm King Art Center
Feed me something else

Aerospace engineer for the U.S. government
Gather your black friend
Listen to cowboys shoot the shit
Lose—no—love your future self

Lay on you Cheez Whiz on a cheesesteak
Dip my card in it
Fux wit my tenderness
Stick me in places like an em dash

Slanderous, insufferable ppl
not invited to the right parties
What that ass do
What them lips do

Catcall yourself b/c you're worth it

What's this nonsense abt a box of chocolates

遇见 ENCOUNTER

——————

You kiss me absentmindedly.

Like you were telling a joke but got bored halfway.
——————

These days it is hard to remain hopeful.
——————

Asking "are you happy now?" like a thermometer, always checking, always broken.
——————

I will never shake this feeling of fraudulence, of insufficiency.
——————

Why is it taboo to project your feelings onto someone, assuming they are worthy?
——————

I grew up in Florida. Pretty much the same area the entire time.
——————

Tan shorts, 5-inch inseam, bad smokes in your double cab Chevy.
——————

I'm filled with a small fear.
——————

You're so cute. Not, like, in a weird way. Just cute.
——————

Your coolness unnerving, you pat me on the back.
——————

We continue our collision, our rift. I love your wretched flesh.

———————

You dive into me, perfect form, no splash. Long lashes & kind rebellion.

———————

You smell like mussels & Neptune.

———————

I'm attracted to a worldview so opposed, so contrary to mine.

I hope it destroys us both.

———————

Push comes to shove, you're a good soldier.

———————

Before you I met two boys named Austin exactly 5 years apart.

They tormented me in different ways.

———————

I want your husk, your honey trap, your cutlet pounded thin as paper.

———————

One of our most beautiful words is *reciprocity*.

———————

Without you I disappear into books, talismans against reality, worlds nicer, ppl kinder.

———————

Suppose some quality of yours, let's say halitosis, causes a man to be lost to you forever.

———————

You say *I'm the smartest person I know.*

I say *less mansplain, more shirtless.*

—————

So funny how you can't ice a cake when it's too hot. Just put it on me already.

—————

Spoil the walls with your steam & cerulean.

—————

This is my 6th shot of espresso. I want to be so woke my heart fuckin bursts.

—————

Deceit aside, you have me. You have me.

—————

Dispose of your friends. You have outgrown them.

—————

You are in a natty bathrobe & I don't care that we're being loud.

—————

You have hair on your shoulder blades & they look like wings.

—————

This is my house, your father says. Yea, I know, daz why the curtains are fuckin hideous.

—————

One time you got mad when I said your father's photos were ugly & that he was a leviathan.

—————

Stop pretending you care abt everything. It's exhausting to watch.

—————

You can never tell the others what I chose.

—————

Time will tell. Will it be truthful?

———————

You were sexier when I knew nothing abt you.

———————

Do you think the stars are more beautiful in the West? From capitalism?

———————

I always confuse OSHA & NOAA. The only bodies I like are bodies of water.

———————

I tell you I don't go to F*re Island b/c Frank O'Hara was martyred there.

———————

$1,000 doesn't buy dick. Do better.

———————

I am so frustrated I dump sand all over the living room floor.

———————

I can't stay at this hotel. I mean I have a certain amount of self-respect.

———————

Buy the house on the water. You have to waste your winnings on something.

———————

We have to separate the wheat from the chaff.

———————

Nothing is agreed to until everything is agreed to.

Everything is negotiable until it isn't.

———————

You just wanted answers all the time, & I'm more a cross-that-bridge kinda gal.

———————

Wack ass whiteboys & their head games.

––––––––––

Is there some ugly truth, some nagging reality that you've never admitted?

Like how you do this for the power & not the greater good?

Is it alarming how the oysters shimmer like they know your secret?

––––––––––

Here's some trivia, some little-known fact: your favorite boy loves you.

––––––––––

The motive of it all is promiscuity.

––––––––––

I know more abt pussy than Tracy Chapman.

––––––––––

Newspapers give me anxiety. I read them for the comics.

––––––––––

Ppl will protest anything but no one bats an eye at the Evil Law Firm.

––––––––––

Your music is so bad even Kidz Bop won't tolerate it.

––––––––––

The most dangerous place in D.C. is between Chuck Schumer & a camera.

But no one get in between Cody & his bubble tea.

––––––––––

Hi, do you work here?

A horrible silence.

––––––––––

What a sweet gift this is, this memory, your pale blue trunks hanging to dry.

———————

It's hard to accept ppl for who they are.

Indiscretions smoothed over when we were younger tend to flare up, come roaring back.

———————

If I believe in America's destiny, what does it mean for my own?

———————

Language me a poem under 6 pages.

———————

Hunter asks why I eat so many cherry cough drops.

I like how his pale cheeks flush with color, how his hair changes with the light.

I'm giddy. I blink, not answering.

I want to be the colors in your throat, Hunter says.

———————

How well do you know the city you live in?

Do you know all the nooks & crannies, the places that delight & spark joy?

———————

Don't worry child, you're well on your way to becoming a statistic.

———————

Together the queers feast on lamb chops & strenuously propagate the species.

———————

Listening to Mariah Carey is gay, the whiteboy says to the exchange student.

He repeats the last word, stretching it out, satisfied with himself.

His hair is brown & wavy & his nose is small & upturned, like a pug's.

That night, they fuck, codes broken, letting their hips do the talking.

———————

One time I asked Jason Schwartzman what he was up to.

He said *you know, pretending to be other ppl.*

———————

Did I say "poem"? I meant life.

•

SEVEN NATION ARMY

Dear Saint Beach Boy: I was minding my own business when you landed in my lap like a runaway meatball. You are resplendent, old-timey like pressed flowers in an album.

You must be wondering how I came to know your name. I put my prodigious skills to the task of identifying you, marking you like an animal, making you mine, a deer with a tracking implant.

I like the shape of your head. You have a barely-suppressed grin of entitlement, like you saved the world. Understandable, I suppose, since you look just like the servicemen in old photographs, victorious Grade-A beefcakes. There are ugly ones, of course, short faces, horse faces, God-pinched faces. But yours is a classic beauty, a reminder that handsome is eternal, hormones alive and well.

From here your hair looks strawberry blonde and luscious. I wonder if it feels like hot honey, how it runs through my fingers like sand, sand I bottle and keep in the drawer with the false bottom, a memento for our troubles.

You look vodka-fuelled, carefree, but your eyes are fixed with an incredible intensity, small and black, and I find my throat catching. You wink at your friends and everything seems alright, time is a construct, I feel suspended outside my body. You yell, you're loud, some would say obnoxious, but they don't understand, don't they see the sweat spotlighted on your strong back, the small tufts under your arms, how your toes grip the sand in a gentle caress, I dream of sucking on them, rinsing them first, of course. You feign getting stabbed, eyes big, expression startling yet comical. I find myself leaning forward, partly concerned, fully wanting, although I know it is an illusion, a mirage in the truest sense.

I look for clues in your expression, some trace of your humanity, and am left with an overwhelming sense of longing for something I never knew (and in all likelihood never will). I analyze your furrowed brow, your gestures, the way you lift and tilt your head at an angle, like you're waiting for something to hit. At moments you appear a fortress unto yourself, quick-tempered, I wonder about the strength of your bite and the rigidity of your smile, hoping to be let in on your little secret, I imagine saying something profound to you, it echoes unsteadily but you don't hear me, I consider this a personal failing I'm desperate to cure, a mark of shame I'm manic to conceal.

Truth be told, Saint Beach Boy, I want you no-frills, a 3-starred motel, I don't expect much. My Own Private Idaho, you'll have your hand in my pants soon enough, invasive as a spear, you mutter something under your breath, feverish. Is it the sun or something else?

Your mission, should you choose to accept it, is to please me, keep me entertained, talk to me about waiting in line at Howlin' Ray's just to feel something again. How Phillip was such a good person he showed no emotion when he saw the parking ticket. The throwbackedness of the name Phillip.

The time I was watching a movie and thought the Azn was Vera Wang but my mom said *that is not Vera Wang that is just an average Azn*. About a force field of acoustic guitars and decadent young men consumed by vice. My favorite poets and the way they are mostly very nice people with no bite. My secret bias for the acidic, the edgy, the meow! Why Hole is simply one of the best band names. The acceptability of wearing white to somebody else's wedding. How Jack and Meg were not brother and sister but, in fact, husband and wife. How you'd drink blue milk, glowing so neon, because you'll try anything once. At this my mind wanders.

The way you approach strangers, their eyes widening, something disquieting stirring within them. How you fuck me wearing nothing but a tux shirt with a bibbed front, cufflinks glimmering and catching the light as my toes curl and your knees buckle, our excuse for a little glamor. How I just saw you help a baby shark back into the water.

Your aptitude for sacking me, needful and fleshy, intent on destruction.

Your instincts and reflexes flashing beautifully, free, the airiness and immediacy of it all.

How happy I am, to have something stable now.

Oh. You are waving at me. Oh. You are walking over.

What now?

FISHSTICKS!

"They learn me a tongue / but no cheek to keep it in"—Kevin Young

"I ain't all that innocent but I don't be lookin for nothing I don't deserve"—Ed Roberson

An enjoyable first date is a relationship planting the seeds of its own destruction. Last night, a prophet came to me in a feverish vodka dream.

There is no drunk like Goose drunk, that clear smoothness sliding down your throat: so clean, no shame. Shame like a jar of God's worst jam, you know abt us & shame.

Like Gabriel I'll visit you, lean a little in the heat, reveal to you, welcome your good neck into my life.

목소리 (mogsoli) is Korean for voice

As in 듣고 싶어 너의 그 목소리

.—*I want to hear your voice*—.

I get ready for my slumber party. Caucasian say *look alive*. RJ puts his mouth on it, hums the summer anthem.

You put your foot on the kettle & it's scalding. Everybody wants to rule the world. I want to be humiliated by you.

Updike said the semicolon is the valet of punctuation. Ms Ruefle, I knew Neruda, & you are no Neruda.

67

Ears like fennec fox
Yea baby I'm listening,
Obama at Trump Tower
Didn't Writers of Philly crown you
Most Sonorous & Musically Fit

Mike & Ike: the first candied queers, fruity &
chewy. Great neighbors. *Contra* John & Jaci:
horrible couple, two tubs of cat piss. Jaci the
botched handjob, human equivalent of books
burning. I want to be close to you like cream on
eyelid. Brought to you by Swann Salon.

I'll carry your water, be the [boy]
you've been waiting for brah.

Sarah Manguso may be the new queen
of shade. She said

.—I read another friend's new novel

*Its only flaw is that a hundred other novelists
could have written it—.*

Dam Sarah tell us what you really
think gurl

Cory was seeing someone famous
I read abt that someone's promotion in Page Six
today
Must be weird learning what a notable ex is up to
*I regret to inform you that your ex is doing so well/has
been promoted/won the lottery*
No—fuck you!!!!

I'm a scarab crawling up your tanned
knee, your high-waisted short shorts.
You ask me what I'm up to. I say *you*

know, dismantling the patriarchy, it's abt systems. Scratch the surface, break your skin. *If you're a poet, why haven't I heard of you? Oh, you're Canadian~*

No one ever says *fuck the FDNY*

Skeletor: Send In Trap Jaw & Mer-Man: the NATION must restore ORDER!
Minions stand ready.

"Tom Cotton" is as close to having a Senator named Jim Crow as reality would allow

They're playing professional baseball in front of stuffed animals. This should be a permanent change.

Her name is J.K. cuz this bitch aint serious

The Clown Governor of New Jersey "paying respects" to George Floyd while sitting at Woodrow Wilson's old desk (literally) is peak Jersey. Gabe says *being from Jersey means never having to say you're sorry.*

Strongly suspect Charlie Puth is a problematic Jersey White but I like him. Charlie Hall, Julia Louis-Dreyfus's son, is 6'5" & has a sense of humor/dick the size of Alaska   @_@

Mr Braggadocio do you even know what a ReFi is

First, why is this White man telling me why & how I'm angry? Second, preemptively pledging support to law enforcement is a great way to look stupid when they screw up. Third, instead of gratuitously sighing & handwringing, why doesn't he do his job? Twiddling his thumbs while his city burns; inappropriately interfering with charging decisions. What is he even talking abt?

O.J. Simpson put out a statement on the unrest, says justice has not been served. Lmao!!!! Obama put out a statement. Don't need to read it to know it's weak as fuck.
R— texts me *did you write that*

Rude!   I think abt that a lot

BRIGHT WHITE NOISE

天使脸 • 恶魔心

They say that writers valorize the specific.

When you write "blue collar" or "working class" or "rural," you mean white. Everyone already knows. Just say white.

Oh, you talked to a Pennsylvania/Ohio voter? At a throwback diner? Good for you.

In stories you're often trying to describe something very specific & material, even if it's a state of mind or emotional landscape.

So—sometimes it's more comforting to think of boys as one unattainable monolith.

Boys that blur together into a blob, racially-ambiguous like Keanu.

Boys that touch you in that fleeting way they leave only grief.

Boys dashing between pickups, lanky & lacrosse-playing, making you want to die like the coyotes.

Stories are like real life, I guess, full of bad choices. There are some people you just love to hate.

At Mudd Club we load every rift with ore, Debbie Harry talking that eschatological ultra-talk.

Lust & loins, husky blare of horns, no feedback here.

Punch a hole in rabbit ears, God is not the type to clip their own nails.

Make it count, the fall will break you.

Inspect me. Search my crevices prospector. Mine me golden child. Unearth this unholy pleasure.

What if my body were an idea.

Make it embarrassing, up the ante. More engorged ways of knowing, sympathizing, & keeping at bay.

Fugue state turgidity, swelling.

Funnier, lustier, more important, more graceful, more regal in bearing. Or at the very least more *cheerful*.

I have labored mightily, toiled even, to be your precious feather.

So cool since my sisters must now rear me. You mean "raise." You rear *animals*.

I've been thinking abt the color yellow lately. Chiquita Banana quite possibly the world's most perfect fruit but for the terrorist activity.

All art is in service of the political.

On the corner of White & Cortlandt.

I find you, hair brown, eyes green flecked with gold.

I look up your party registration.

You're speedboats & PBR, I'm chopped liver, chum, & cadaver. Poor man's Pearl Harbor.

Is Ryan Murphy killing off the cast of Glee.

Baby tell me your genealogy, I'll study your family tree, follow your circuitry.

Like Robocop I'll come back even better.

Does memory make identity. What 7 moments in your life define it.

What if you could pick which memories make your identity.

Brain in a jar I remember you sleek, muscly, tragic. I want you to do odd, unspeakable things.

Fuck remembrance. I want to forget.

What if the pt of life was to make one person happy.

Is that person me.

Your sleep-talk totally coherent & ruthlessly compassionate, you check if I'm okay even in your dreams.

You simplify the world, make stuff make sense.

You erase my general uneasiness with boys, make the strange ones leave me alone.

You tug your dick & create the White Album, touch your junk propellant.

You arrive sure as officer-involved shooting, smelling expensive like oud.

If you were a sexy calendar you'd be all the months.

You're so sexy you're all the zodiacs, a heap of frantic beasts.

You know perfectly well that shubunkins are Japanese goldfish, always return the rental with a full tank.

You always respond to emails from your academic advisor who totally has the hots for you but then again who wouldn't.

You live rent-free in my brain, a second home you can claim anytime you want.

I wonder what lurks behind those maple eyes, unwavering but hinting at sadness.

I want to be your great dragon hurled down, from Earth I'll lead the world astray.

I watch thoughts unfold across your face. *Be patient with me*, you say, *I've only done this with girls—*.

You play around with me in your mouth, a little unsure. Pop me in & let your tongue investigate, salivary glands working overtime. My flesh dissolving, you push on the meaty bits clinging to my puckered pit, satisfied.

I'm bad at describing the things that strike me the most deeply.

What does your Chinese girlfriend do. She is, well, *homely*.

Does she kiss your dull, drunk anus with feeling. Is she capable of feeling, I know how they are.

You expertly rotate your tongue, loosening my muscles like gears in a vault. The lock clicks open & I taste tropical. You say *I could get used to this*. I muster the strength to nod, trusting your delightful buoyancy completely.

I tell you I had sex with a famous poet, the one really talented with their line breaks.

I hold you like fragile knick-knacks from Pearl River Mart, statue of Guanyin with droopy eyes.

I watch you fold your laundry, veins dancing. I kiss your chiseled flesh, my hands hellhounds ravaging your body in a f*ggy parody.

I have a hard time imagining you angry but you fill me with such dread.

I've never left your womb or these parentheses, I am Apes & you are Planet Of The. A pebble in your space.

Tell me your secrets, your Damita Jo, your Robin Wright Penn.

I push your hair back, caress your tresses.

Speak deadly to me, exquisite corpse.

Again—. With emotion this time—.

I starved myself, ready for your stink, rank like old beer.

Shoes on, my own retch, girlfriend watching, you begging *please*—.

Spread you like herpes at a state school.

Buoyed by currents, soft moans push from your throat.

Ugh, I can't bear to look—.

DRAKKAR NOIR

"and what i want to know is / how do you like your blue-eyed boy / Mister Death"
—e. e. cummings

_____, take a look around. Last I heard, the world kept coming. My debt makes it too expensive to _____. The police are the public & the public are the police. My _____ doesn't know _____ has never been so easy. Under penalty of law, I've been taking my loneliness as

Fatty feral children

Good clothes but hideously self-hating

Baffled by the question abt occasional poems

Occasion as in special event

Not once-in-a-blue-moon

Yes, I suppose I do write the occasional poem, I said

What's it to you?

I used to find the concept of rereading a book so foreign

Alien almost

I've started doing it, & not even for books I particularly like

I wonder if this means I am old & white now

I've been thinking abt my book cover,

how advised it would be to use the color scheme of a failed airline,

if an aircraft crashing & burning would taint my book

Taint as in the narrow strip between genitals & asshole

I read somewhere that our taste buds dull as we age

I remember watching the aging French actor

staring as he wolfed down steak tartare & freedom fries

wrinkly & disgusting

Later in life I find myself ordering steak tartare as a treat

My dulled taste buds wanting that sinewy rawness

The hot sting of fries burning the fuck outta my mouth

The seared roof tender but quick-healing

Look how careful, how sensible I am

Like a draft dodger or DIET MOUNTAIN DEW

I laugh abt the period of Australian political turbulence

where they had so many changes in government

It was no longer reliable to ask a wakening patient

Who is the Prime Minister?

For a week I've done nothing but recite TLC lyrics

Don't go chasing waterfalls . . .

I took a job b/c I liked a boy

He quit the next day

Meaning he quit me

So I promoted myself

Uncoordinated like octopus

Let's go all the way / tonite

Baraka said "never let Mr. Chan send you into a dark room by yourself"

I think he meant Detective Charlie Chan

In any case, it's pretty good advice

Prophet to profit

Dawn to dusk

24 시간 (24 HOURS)

ALWAYS HAVE A STORY
BAIT LIKE THE BUS
STAGED BUT I DON'T CARE
EXALT IN THEIR BODIES
WORTHLESS BOYS
DECORATE YOUR PLAIN
WHINNYING THROAT EXPLOSION
WILLIWAW OF CUM
LOAD IN DIAL-UP
CASTING COUCH BATED BREATH
POISON BY MAKE-UP
QUEST TO LOOK WHITE
WAIT FOR IT
THERE ARE MANY PEOPLE AT VERSAILLES TODAY
BUT NO PLUMBING
CAN YOU IMAGINE THE SMELL
BLOND PATROCLUS SWEAT LIKE HONEY
DOES THAT MAKE ME VENUS BEAUTIFUL
POUR GOLD KNOCK SCALES OFF BALANCE
CREATIVE HOLLYWOOD ACCOUNTING
I DON'T KNOW HER ACHILLES
THE RESEMBLANCE IS UNCANNY LOUIS MAYER
TITANS OF INDUSTRY MAKE AMUSING PETS
GREAT PHYSIQUE (PHI-SEKKKKS) LAZY EYE
DISMISSED AS TRADE
EUREKA BETTA PUT SOME RESPEK ON IT
PLUM AS PEACH
YOU TASTE SO LEMONY
MASTURBATED BY
THE LONG ARM
OF COINCIDENCE
THEY TELL ME
NO TRANS FATS

道听途说 RUMORS

When an Azn editor accepts one of my poems, a fellow poet says: "You guys can be poo poo platter together." Yea we'll make you moo goo gai pan. How food fuses consumption & identity. How the act of eating is erotic & violent. How I once promised to swallow John like an eclair, wholly consuming his confection. Lately I've been obsessed with being enough for a boy. One specific boy. One boy in particular. One boy whose nakedness I'm curious abt. Phil Dunphy said that success is 1% inspiration, 98% perspiration, & 2% attention to detail. I wonder what will be enough for this boy. How queerness is a vector & not a destination. 80% of life is showing up. I'm showing up for your body. It is very satisfying to call someone a *******. The way the word swirls in your mouth like a fine whiskey & comes out silky smooth. I mean the word fremder, German for "stranger." Eating makes me vulnerable. How race is a fishbone in the throat. How I want to be a lost tampon between your scarecrow's thighs, meeting you when you come through. How you couldn't masturbate after moving back in with your mom. Untouched Vaseline, high on a shelf somewhere, out of sight & away from inquisitive eyes. Sometimes you show me glimpses of the real you. I want to pierce the veil. Eat you peskily. Pay tribute to your visual culture. A political act. My body is inscribed with the marks of race, & food, & you. Tell me what you eat & I shall tell you what you are. We are all chameleons in our diet, salamanders in our habitat, inasmuch as we live always in the fire of our own smoldering combustion. Last night I dreamt that you'd written me. But of course you hadn't. I want to smear my smile onto your face. Share the standard Chinese greeting: "吃饭了吗?" "Have you eaten?" How we sense our own fear. Slip out of our half-underground apartment. Drive past the sign. Avert our gaze. Get trashed like the Bush twins. Yea I tend to think that we'll be together again. You got to burn to shine. A baby puffin is called a puffling. Nutella is pronounced "new-tell-uh," not "NUT-tella." I want to nut in the first Canadian that comes to mind. There is no such thing as permission cheese. If I get dragged out of here in cuffs, Bruce, what do you think my last act would be?

非凡 EXCEPTIONAL

Delicate like a poached egg, he asks:
Do you know America's secret, leaning in
I stare back blankly
The more you love her, the more she loves you back,
he slumps in his chair, satisfied with himself
I stare some more, distracted
By his, I don't know, manly ambition
We don't break eye contact
In my head I'm saying
Don't slow the proceedings,
I object to a continuance
We ravish one another

Most ppl are lost, some are just better at hiding it than others
Yes umwelt our messy entanglements & conscious uncouplings

It's funny how ppl were saying that the peaches in Parasite
were some serious motif & symbolism of prosperity's toxicity
In actuality Bong Joon-ho had a classmate with a peach allergy
& he incorporated it into the film
Which goes to show how much of life is bullshit & buffoonery
& how little critics actually know

Poetry for the miracles
Like the one who left, coming back
I want to need him: sex familiar & unfussy
Am I your 친구 (chingu)?
Poetry for the cures to the saddest words
"I want what they have"
"I could love you but I don't"
"I don't love you anymore"
Poetry for the fixes
I'm commandeering this vehicle
I intend to arrive

THE SAN VICENTE BUNGALOWS

~   ~

Secret society called the Cat's Paw   fellow travellers & tragic queen Akhmatova
       I don't remember when I found God   but recall the first time I laid eyes on KJ Apa
It's impolite to say "blind barber" these days   they prefer "blind hairdresser"

       Don't waste your time asking   spend your time doing
If you're not moving   you're falling behind
       Last of the English Roses   parents reincarnated as children

       Raise me to your mouth   Batty boi   show off your batty shus
they're Gucci   snapped up inna jiffy   innit

I love you like a fat kid love cake   feed me my favorite lies I mean lines
If only I had iron bands strapped around my heart   to keep it from breaking   I wish I were
grey cliffs   a heart-shaped lake on Pluto   no longer a planet   illusive like justice

Tell me abt the lonely boat   elusive like remembering   hedgehogs disguised as chocolates
       I tolerate woodpeckers   I hate running out of breath   I have always loved the gaps
the spaces between things   as much as the things   I dissolve in you like the fizzy water tablets
popularized in the 80s   taste my lactose intolerance   you're unlucky like the Lao
the idiot white cops handed right back to   Jeffrey Dahmer   Ray Antrobus won the
Geoffrey Dearmer Prize   Clare wants to know abt the lizard brain   the lizard testified abt
Benghazi for 11 hrs   English the language of oppression   to be perfectly honest
       I'm tired of the violence

Erasure is lazy like you   your manuscript repetitive & dull   bloated & forgettable
stale & smug   unbelievably dour & boring   Holy sweet chili & tea-smoked duck
       there are no insights to be found here

Coulda been a frat boy   coulda been a nightmare   stump of cat
Queerer than Abe[]   Guiltier than Cain   you ask if T.S. Eliot was the undercover womxn
In the future white supremacy will not need white ppl   laughing so hard at Keith S. Wilson's line
       see the corona of your face   talk abt unfortunate   Azn lady broke up the Beatles
Funny how the British say clerk   like "clark" like Kent like Bruce's boots

82

I cut my hair to resemble a tomboy   I don't like how my name sounds
coming from his mouth   weak & uncertain   His lips of sweet clover
          gaslighting bastard tongue   perfect for praise & obligatory heterosexuality
Lingering over my vowels   well-intentioned but missing the mark   I am his mark
Barging in on somebody else's meet cute   I'm worried no fearful he'll say *ching chong* next
He'll be tempted to tell me what I already know   Transfixed by his sound
consonants hanging precariously   mouth a delicate assembly   I bathe in his syllables
love his intimate access point   ah yes   Rosencrantz & Guildenstern are dead

What does it mean to live   I don't believe in coming clean   but I think of you often
I can't hear you   come in the water   tell me what's good   pull me into black

Suppose a curfew   suppose a window   suppose a mattress   suppose a breeze
suppose scorpions in a bottle   suppose butterflies in a mason jar   hey you missed a spot

~   ~

CHINATOWN ROMEO

I observe John taking a shit

      (it stinks really bad)

I don't tell anyone what I witness

      (it reeks so bad)

He isn't a vegetarian

      —do you think he's ashamed?

Is that why he's trolling the

      corridors, catching glimpses of

      transitory boys in towels?

   Shuffling boys with no souls,

  the outlines of their bulges fastidious

   Floppy cocks in

        various guises,

     pricks a nourishing sight

One so beautiful John drops his laptop

    —howling

Scattering boys like cockroaches

    despoiled & accidentally awake

BETTER WITH THE LIGHTS ON

sweet thing • don't u know • dreams always start in diners • 君子之交淡如水 • stupid boy says he's with her, it's true, but he's in the room most of the day • he's working remotely, doesn't do anything • he swears he just wants a change of scenery • stupid boy i waited for u by the tennis courts but u never showed • u didn't, wouldn't, pick up • stupid sheep boy u are not my lamb • ur mediocre, poetically speaking • yr dull blink, somewhere else • yr voice agreeable like thunder • u taste like jerky & tears • ideal model to pose in the altogether • yr arms hairy like dungeness crab • the degree of civilization in a society judged by entering its 7-elevens • i wish u'd said something • i'm a one-hit-wonder but i'll make u cum twice • moneyshots & dollar-store royalties • rip it up & start again • i'm a heat-seeking missile for mistakes • move fast, break things • u addict of the basic • junkie of the banal • i'm tired of watching u trespassed upon • sick of being engulfed by u • as if love & honor mattered (pretend) • never underestimate the power of a shared look, a shy glance • *i like to go on drives, clear my head* • he might as well have said he enjoyed salsa dancing, or caring for bonsai, things i know nothing about • i learned to number my moods • each a waypoint • teaching me to unpack his thirst • sensual like peeling an orange • don't know the emperor of ice cream but i'll lick yr orange creamsicle • my chinese tongue turned state's witness • no translation necessary • his fingers fixed to my head, keying the car to my soul • love me fat like brando • sop up my inner filth • an adult trauma to cover a baby trauma • back when we didn't have a name for it • i knew enough to count it as a blessing • a gentleman's friendship, insipid as water • u never tell me when u feel small • why is that • u taught me intense disembodiment • the size of onigiri • the salt • swim laps yr lips are blue • there are two wolves • whiteboys & lies • i feed u • i feed u • i feed u • i feed u until it is too much • u trying to one-up the night • all macho irritating but correct murphy's law • i'm yr idol's idol • the yo-yo ma of ego-stroking • push u out of my life like a big turd • forgive myself & make up games to pass the time • i have to know the entire life of a story & it must be a single breath • i'll give u a romance plucked from the headlines • offer a prayer to the small god of hindsight • dream u so treacly • nirvana when i do that thing u like • who needs solace when we have solange • my little heart fast like a rabbit's • why u gotta be so rude • have u considered homeownership • gravity galaxy • untamed planets • pulling me towards u density of light • 念念不忘 • 江湖 • rivers & lakes • around the whole country • u have an unused prime benefit

SKIN IN THE GAME

My summer's beer in frosted mugs, older boys in high-waisted shorts, so short they require constant rearrangement, my summer's Meatless Mondays, Jordache jeans, Basquiat on my chest, frozen pizzas in the freezer, my summer's love, attracted to things that terrify them

Your compliments as infrequent as Manhattanhenge, we down Bloody Marys, watch Lady Liberty on this sizzling marble seat, road-worn trucks slide towards us, your boat slamming into my dock, what are they saying on social media

Your teeth rose gold, you put your lips on me, to the mouth that doesn't speak, I don't know how to quit, but why would I, when I'm ahead, tell me, it's love isn't it

I was 30 years old when I found out what Pasta Raphael was, Raphael the sarcastic & hot-tempered turtle, the accidental vegetarian, full of tomatoes, artichokes, garlic, & onion

Boy, I like your focaccia thick & generous with olive oil & sea salt, I like your heft, let it drop, hang low from its weight, remind me who you are & why you are here

NIGERIAN PRINCE

he had bad skin

i had some chinese herbs to clear it up

he was worried that someone had seen the video

the video of him casually walking by

hands in his pockets

unbothered by the horror unfolding in front of him

maybe even a smirk on his face

what would it mean for his political career

honey badger

all you write abt is bone broth & anal

the hacks on this zoom are not the future

white ppl high off their own fumes

dude named prior i think *to wut!*

i'll make you an offer you can't refuse

lick you like flames

support you like pillow

i'll take you there

POEM ENDING WITH LINES
FROM FRANK O'HARA

"I have seen boys, also, walk in the street with their arms twined around each other's necks, and always in each other's society. They say they love each other very much."—Jena Osman

"As a dog returns to his vomit, so a fool repeats his folly"—Proverbs 26:11

———

In 1467, Alfonso de Spina asserted that
the number of demons was
133,316,666

Living in Brooklyn is Napoleonic exile

I'm the Pope of desire
like fucking with the weather

Like a storm
taking a bath in seltzer

With dry eyes
watch my heart harden
Evan & his practice tests

———

I hate ppl asking who I write for

I don't write for myself

I do other things for myself

I do this for you

—

You the whiteboy whisperer
Pied Piper of questioning boys
I want to be the type of bitch who sips tea & sits
    on chintz
I think it's bad there are giraffes in New Jersey—
giraffes shouldn't have to deal with that

—

You get off on his hiking pics,
rub your bean to him, rhythmically

Tell him you want to see his mountaintop
His cock bends towards white supremacy

He returns to the Appalachian trail
He will get his comeuppance

                                              —

                                              Sextina sestina cat's in
                                                    the cradle Hanoi
                                              Jane

                                              Comedy is tragedy
                                                    plus time

                                              LANA TURNER
                                              HAS
                                              COLLAPSED!

                                              oh Lana Turner we
                                              love you get up

HIGH DRAMA PANDA FURY

A fougère is a scent designed to mimic how a fern smells
Easy, obvious, straightforward enough, except ferns don't really have smells
So a fougère is someone's IDEA of what a fern OUGHT to smell like
. . . nobody dies in this poem b/c dying is not cute

Not all boys are worth chasing
I want to be ambitious yet cowardly
Yes it is better to lie in wait
You are cordially invited to cuddle with me, panting heroically:

Yes I want to have nice legs
I want to be tired after practice
I want to have muscles shapely & intimidating
I want to arouse envy

I want to taste artificially flavored blueberry
I want to have never seen Jurassic Park
I want to be unburdened by the knowledge of Jeff Goldblum as sex symbol
I want to be relieved that Chris Pratt is str8

I want to be from Long Island
I want to brunch with Her Majesty's Most Loyal Opposition
I want to catfish the Lieutenant Governor of California
I want to discuss the lady ghostbusters with my lady lawyer

I want to write a poem abt a horse
I want to know where to hide a body
I want to be lost at sea
I want to be one with the otters

I want to speak one language
I want to be Alan Cumming's bathrobe
I want to catch the burglar in the act
I want to kiss him mid-tantrum

Yes I want to call in a favor with the moon
Hey
You there
Have you learned nothing

YANKEE YELLOW

§ § §

Yankee Yellow problem officer Yankee Yellow Commie scum Yankee Yellow poo poo platter Yankee Yellow Yoo-hoo diet Yankee Yellow big appetite Yankee Yellow global warming Yankee Yellow evil cow Yankee Yellow tunnel vision Yankee Yellow man-made error Yankee Yellow shoot Rumpelstiltskin Yankee Yellow regime change Yankee Yellow continental divide Yankee Yellow strange & lovely Yankee Yellow sour cream & onion Yankee Yellow chandelier tinkle Yankee Yellow fentanyl stutter Yankee Yellow New Rochelle Yankee Yellow Amish Mafia Yankee Yellow Bunny Ranch Yankee Yellow Christian amateur Yankee Yellow hands full of hair Yankee Yellow split ends Yankee Yellow bursting at the seams Yankee Yellow Pet Detective Yankee Yellow lonely prophet Yankee Yellow October surprise Yankee Yellow Santo Domingo Yankee Yellow Atlas Shrugged Yankee Yellow Panda Express Yankee Yellow Darndest Things Yankee Yellow intern me daddy Yankee Yellow freshman fifteen Yankee Yellow sophomore slump Yankee Yellow Occam's razor Yankee Yellow Oppen's G-string Yankee Yellow Tim Burton's Rocketman Yankee Yellow Push by Sapphire Yankee Yellow executive summary Yankee Yellow remember or forget Yankee Yellow Five Guys Five Eyes Yankee Yellow one poem one page Yankee Yellow aliens or ghosts Yankee Yellow Christmas morning Yankee Yellow ugly pidgin Yankee Yellow unrimmed holes Yankee Yellow spick & span Yankee Yellow content warning Yankee Yellow quick & dead Yankee Yellow mad scientist Yankee Yellow solar-powered coat Yankee Yellow full of treason Yankee Yellow Chinese Wall Yankee Yellow over easy Yankee Yellow Jeremy Lin Yankee Yellow last laugh Yankee Yellow close to God Yankee Yellow without a trace

§ § §

OPIUM

Galoshes

Anything for the chase

Blue blue fin

Blue blue tuna

Love like Babylon

Swallow

This lake of fire

This nest of spit

FIELD NOTES ON THE PRODIGAL SON

she knows before i do that i want you

they see us out at dinner, dressed in our finery

i'm in a leather jacket from charivari

i don't remember what you're wearing, it's the 80s

* * *

we order duck confit & baked alaska

not knowing what to expect

they say *what a pretty family*

too bad they are chinks

升天 SKYBOUND

b r o o k l y n b u t a n i k u d o u b l e m e a n i n g s y o u k n o w f u n n y l a n g u
a g e p e r f o r m i n g p i l f e r i n g p h i l a n d e r i n g y o u k n o w t o a c c o u n
t f o r w o r d p o v e r t y g i n g h a m c h e c k s l u s h g a r d e n s r a l p h l a u r e
n f l a g s w e a t e r s t o n g u e s f a t b r a i n s f o g g y f r o m c h a m p a g n e b
o d i e s b l o a t e d f r o m a f o r e m e n t i o n e d s a u s a g e s o n l i t t l e t o o
t h p i c k s a p r i v a t e s o r t o f t a s t e i c a n s a f e l y s a y y o u h a v e n e v e r
e x p e r i e n c e d a n y t h i n g q u i t e l i k e i t c l o s e t o l u s t p r o x i m a t e t
o m a d n e s s n e c k s i n l a p s h a n g i n g b r o k e n b o y f o u n d w a n t i n g
t u g g i n g h i s t h i n g t r u t h b e i n g t h a t s e x i s l y i n g t o g e t h e r l y i n
g t o e a c h o t h e r s w e l l i n g y o u r w o r d p l a y m y t i g h t n e s s f i r s t f i
r e a l m o s t l i k e t h e y w a n t e d i t h o w r i g g e d t h e y s a i d v e r y i b e l i e
v e i n t u i t i o n i n s p i r a t i o n s o m e t i m e s f e e l s r i g h t i d o n o t k n o
w o u r p l a c e o u r h o r r o r s k y b o u n d m e a n i n g h i g h t i d e m e a n i n
g t o o r g a s m p i t y i t d i d n o t l a s t

WE ARE THE PIGS

There was a time Simon thought everything Jude put out in the world was gold: his every breath, every utterance, his every thought evaporating into the ether.

Jude hated being taught anything, he shrank away from anything remotely resembling a lesson or request, he wasn't big on teachable moments, no, those were to be scorned and avoided.

Simon needed somewhere to direct his ample affections, someone to recklessly spoil, an object to admire, a target to pamper without regard for anything else …

Jude was a convenient vessel, he was beautiful, so it was easy to ascribe a flawless personality to him, free of blemishes, to generate a sort of care and concern, a cool gel gliding across a surface.

All Simon could think about was Jude squeezing himself against his body, pressing so much of himself against him … Jude, warm and hairy in his bed …

Jude's wandering eye, so obvious that even Simon realized it, Simon who was used to giving people the benefit of the doubt, overlooking things, granting allowances … it was clear that Jude was distracted.

Simon's greatest fear was that Jude would flip out and say something remorseless and devastating, something he couldn't take back or paper over, and Simon would have a bad time of it. Simon's biggest consolation was that Jude was stand-offish and bored.

Simon often imagined Jude as a fine rum, smooth and delicious and not sticking in his throat, but he doesn't quite remember what Jude looks like anymore, Jude's deceptive nice-boy features fading like foolish trends, traceless as last season's fashions.

The asking and answering, the denial and demand, the mouths, caresses in slow motion, Jude's lips like Cupid's bow, his smelling of expensive soap, the exceptional moans, slow, furious, the sweet tremble, so much and all at once …

Physical closeness was good, as if the proximity alone was a cure-all, a guarantee, Simon almost enjoyed watching Jude's mask slip on and off, the voice never changing, what little personality Jude revealed punctuating their conversations …

Simon liked Jude's voice hard, bordering on cruel, his macho attractive and the source of boundless fantasy, his face icy, impassive, his approval difficult and rare …

Simon felt like a pink eraserhead, not exactly essential, there but not certain when (if) he would be called into play …

When it came to loyalty, Simon was a swan and Jude a thieving blue jay. Ironically, Simon took pleasure in serving Jude, it was a timid sort of confidence, an almost triumphant attitude that temporarily assuaged concerns over Jude's loyalty and attention span.

It was a claiming, but not the kind of obsessive ownership that befalls most relationships, Jude was slippery and Simon knew it. Simon was generally calm on the surface but knots would tighten in his stomach. Jude regarded everything acidly. Simon tried to grin and bear it, pretending Jude's fleeting attention and texts were little gifts to be treasured, morsels packed with flavor that lasted until the next batch arrived (who knew when). When the mood struck, Jude could be effusive in his praise, and Simon could be convinced, even moved, by these casual, meaningless overtures …

Simon always felt like he was watching Jude at a remove, like he was seeing Jude for the first time and from a distance. It was almost tranquil, the waiting, the (he hated to say) coming in from the cold … Jude's laughing things off in the face of Simon's absurd hope, Simon's forced recognition that Jude was in control, he had always been in control, ceding nothing, even when he'd appeared to relinquish it for brief moments, it was only a ploy to get Simon to come closer, perfect, there you go, good boy.

Simon often felt like he was wandering the deep hallways of a vast palace, sleepwalking, almost, with no destination in mind, but to be technical Jude was the kind of boy who came and went, noiseless but capable of tugging at heartstrings with a surgeon's precision, a sorcerer able to bend events to his will, so deeply imprinting himself into your noggin it was impossible to focus on anything else.

It was all thoughtless, instinctive, abrupt, and Jude was a willing recipient of Simon's attention, closing his eyes, sighing a little, jawline impeccable, unmistakably a stud, a champ, swaddled in the softest velvet, velvet snatched off the back of some vanquished king, yes, truth is, everyone has a plan until they get punched in the face.

STRANGE FRUIT

My only Tatum , Channing , j'ai toujours su que tu viendrais

I have no idea what Stevie Wonder's Superstition sounds like, I assume like shit

I am shopping for slippers & run into Verdine White from the Hall of Fame band Earth, Wind & Fire. He says *hi I am Verdine White from Earth, Wind & Fire, have you heard of me?* I say *you need the Oxford comma in there, my dude.* He licks his lips like a cartoon wolf, tries to touch me, & I run away

White readers love Minority writers. If anything the danger lies in writing *too white—* white readers will demand more exotic, more ethnic material

Excuse me, flying witch is a person too, she has a name

My life is just whiteboys saying *my bad* over & over again

My constant anxiety is a poem trying to claw its way out

Jennifer Hate Hewitt

So funny how a R*th L*lly finalist repeatedly & snidely referred to *my language* in my poetry & asked me to take it out ???? In case it wasn't clear, she was talking abt Chinese

I know I'm not supposed to like Tom Holland but vanilla wafers

Boy asks what the scariest book I've ever read is, I say Cujo although I've never read it, I say it to impress him, he says if I was his professor maybe he'd like English more, I am a good literary citizen after all

Another boy expresses an interest in me but I'm on the fence abt him, he goes to night school b/c he is (I imagine) middle class, I wonder what he'll say if I take him to that Italian place Rihanna likes, the one with shitty food but is very sceney

We are at a bar, he looks expectantly at me, asks if I know what *redrum* is, ready to reveal the answer like I haven't seen the Shining a million times, I went to liberal arts school, for heaven's sake

What do skeletons order at a Chinese restaurant? Fried lice. Sorry, I mean spare ribs. They order spare ribs

Someone says my poems are a series of roasts & I feel seen

A lot of poets write for shock value but I am genuinely shocking

Small Tech so small it disappears

O rly u r reading Dune ????

My boy is a tumbleweed

What's your problem?

NOBODY'S EYES BUT MINE

Trickster feminism & truffle butter

You keep saying the city is big & scary
Are you imagining life with me

You like safe & comfortable
You greenhouse little flower

I don't have a clothes chair
I have clothes couch & clothes floor

Stop making me break all the rules for you
Be my impenetrable KITT

Don't poke the bull if you don't want the horns
Be like a foal, birthed & ready to go

I'm feeling you up like the men & the elephant
A happiness when I eat you

Our state bird is murder
My language hurrying to keep up

If sorry is the hardest word
Where does that leave scat

CNF is lies

Poetry is lies

Gender is lies

I am bubble tea

Suck my balls

COUTURE FOR SINNERS

suppose we're thriving despite being impaled by a chair / i retain the powerful image of you biting down on me / my shoulders hurt, i've marked the softest spots / you have the saggy sad face of a belgian malinois past its prime / in for a surprise when i say i'm taking you out for sundae / & we show up at a korean blood sausage restaurant / mansplain me doomsday clock / so sexy & broken / brave as kerfuffle / biscuits in a cup / fuckable fuck boy / chitter chitter in your white voice / show me how to enunciate / i have a tenuous relationship with words / you save your cruelest put-downs for me / or do i have that backwards / have you fixed your hooves / you call me young lord / i hear slumlord but don't correct you / i'll be your agony aunt / total wax figure / smooth & plastic in the front / my idea of abstraction is losing your number / the barn locking itself shut / white ppl are wrong when they're like / *ooooooooooooo trump doesn't even have a dog* / like that's why he's defective / [bush had dog!] / my nipples are sensitive like a fig turned inside out / meanwhile ppl are unstimulated & starving / what ur dog name winston / come on, don't look so anguished / my italian roommate loves to lounge around in his underwear / the crotch is very generous, if you catch my drift / this is where the sperm meets the _____ [tostada] / there won't be a next time / butter knife gone land o'lakes girl missing / it's impolite to say cowboys & indians / they much prefer the term ranchers / ann taylor takes me home in a lincoln town car / hanging onto my every utterance / rich ppl choose heinz red wine vinegar / fuck here i am / lucky like a rabbit's foot dusted with angels

ADVERSE POSSESSION

•

Nobody:
Absolutely nobody:
Poets: SELF-PORTRAIT AS

•

I title my longest poem "Size Queen" until I write one even longer. Now it's "Fake Billionaire Tears"

•

I sign shit "in solidarity—" but never say with what. Answer is me. In solidarity with me.

•

A lot of y'all claim to be from elsewhere but I know ur from Jersey

•

If I read another piece that begins with any etymology, but especially the origins of the word "essay"—

•

Oh yeah ???? How many blacklists are YOU on ????

•

I don't know why ppl say stupid things & then go "that's just my two cents." Well your cents aint worth shit

•

Some poems you read & are like well that's 3 minutes I'm never getting back

•

Remember when ppl thought tech was progressive? That was a fun 20 years

•

Best advice is to get a second opinion. Or learn how to layer, make a mean G&T. For once I just want Snapple caps to tell the truth

•

Millennials are bland btw is Robin Thicke still cancelled

•

What if some of my poetic ancestors are idiots

•

One of Obama's dumbest quotes (which he stole from Rahm) is "never let a good crisis go to waste." Horrible for public policy, but great for poetics!

•

Debates don't matter unless you choke

•

Is Lee Pace just a 6'5" figment of our imaginations or—

•

Don't know what the hell the platinum plan is but I want it

•

I need a workplace that RESPECTS & ADMIRES my jewel-toned knits

•

If the title is longer than the body of the poem you are onto something

•

I feel your pain cuz growing up we only had one (1) car elevator

•

Remember when ppl said Matthew Dickman was the new Frank O'Hara ???? Haha

•

Q has been ax whether art "should" reflect the life we want for ourselves & the world we want to live in. Framed that way, no, art can be anything you want. Just so happens that MY poems are candid abt calling out unjust practices while having fun. Life is short, blow shit up

•

A poem unfurls then manages to coil back up again like a reverse music box

•

Hyper focused, he clips his toenails, massages his feet, rubs his eyes, makes a sandwich

•

Let me see those baby blues, all my life I've ordered grilled cheeses, wanted to be stranded on the great grilled cheese highway, no ketchup in my meatloaf, only jungle fever

•

These feelings, passed thru dat illusive centrifuge, lead to ???? [nowhere], my presence is a gift

●

If you mention birds in poems you will have hairy palms
Who among us hasn't wished for a yacht with a sexy crew ????
Have we sent Nate Silver back under the bridge yet ????
My roommate said Brendan Fraser decided this election

●

"Write what you know" is lazy

●

Someone actually said "big sag energy" to me & I had to say *Nothing saggy—I am TAUT*

●

I saw Kay "Bailout" Hutchison hit a VERY pretty male staffer with a purse as he cowered. I felt so powerful

●

hey blake →
i put up with your adverse possession b/c you're the best lay →
that's how things work →
i'll be on my knees when i'm knighted →
don't check my ID, you're no spring chicken →
sure, we can discuss the strawberries in the bowl →
the girl with the pink notebook →
you boast abt your luck, your luster, _____ , _____ →
i watch you turn in the shadows →
admire your extremities →
you always want the first word—& the last →
somehow →
you believe the stories they tell you →
shake your fat bottle of pills →
push pancakes into my mouth →
i know it's not, you know, orthodox →

but i need to prove something →
i don't know what →
a boy like you wouldn't understand →
if i looked like you my life would be very different →
i hope you'll see me the way i want—
a paper boat in the face of a massive wave →

●

hey blake →
i know better now →
i will never jump the turnstile for you →
i will never drag my shit thru a crowded station for you →
i will never schlep to _____ & _____ for you →
i will never ride a peter pan (or, worse, _____) for you →
go back to your stupid ex-girlfriend →
what have you done for me lately →

●

hey blake →
this could be your lucky day →
tell me →
are you coming or going →

R'D V'LV'T

Hello

I hope this finds you well, given everything that's happened

I like your jumper—very Jeffrey Dahmer

I don't know what to do with that

I believe it is called a retweet

Stop encouraging attractive ppl—we are doing fine

I am happy, grateful to be here, I got your fix

I used your tea leaves to rid the closet of your bad smells

Best of luck with your future endeavors

It is always the kumbaya scum that turn out to be the most evil

Why all poetry blurbs sound sarcastic af

A lot of ppl write pretty words but don't say shit

"Forced universal homosexuality"? Not the ugly ones

When the Dolls said "I hang up the phone, you call me back," the nation felt that

Trump gon name Lee Iacocca his recount czar

"Lauren Bush Lauren" is a real person

White lady rushes to tell me Hotel Rwanda is her feel-good movie

Why does the Tony Blair Institute of anything exist?

Have you considered Fake Billionaire Tears?

What's something that ISN'T antisemitic but FEELS antisemitic to you? MILEY CYRUS

Someone told me Lachlan Murdoch paid Tom Cruise a million dollars for sex & it was still less of a waste than the $200m NC Senate race

He meant what he said. Why is it so hard to understand? Believe fascists the first time blah blah—

I have perfected the art of note-writing & am ready to be a professional housewife

I don't like those pics of hunting or fishing. Cruel

Sports metaphors are violence

She blew her gasket when I said that all monks do is shit & eat, shit & eat

Do you think a donkey knows it's not a horse?

I was in Venice admiring the sunset & trying to get a good angle when the sun disappeared on me

Have you ever seen dogs run in the rain?

Why boys who can't spell—Nic, Wil—usually cute :,) :'(

They give you comfort, make eyes at you when their gf's not looking

You want one for same-sex fucking but it isn't likely so you marry his sister

You acknowledge that they look alike if you squint, yearn for the way his gaze diminishes you

You imagine what he'd look like dislocated from comfort, shiny nails filed down, rounded, draped in black polish or maybe the word you're looking for is *disgorged*, illicit gains to be returned, somebody made whole

You consider his hands, their withholding, how hands, his especially, have stories to tell

You realize there's a lot he doesn't know, so much you could teach him

You learn to recognize the slap-slap of his flip-flops, commit his sounds to memory

You say *I really like this place, thanks for showing me*, he smiles, says *no, it's nothing, you're just hungry*

You feel out of place, like Yeti on a balance beam, detect sadness in his smile

Is he sad b/c he's with you or b/c of the conditions under which you're together?

If your pain is indescribable, have you really felt it?

If he kisses you as he takes your life, would it have been worth it?

Bang bang! Unsalvageable

SOPHOMORE SLUMP

"My dawg would probably do it for a Louis belt"—Drake

●

vain & stupid
he announced he was impotent
when he meant *omnipotent*
we laughed savagely in his beautiful face

warm huddle low-key wanted him
breathless & breezy
bee sting treated with rose water
though hand-holding is miscegenation

show me your familiar ass
skin soft suck on me like a juicebox
push my insides around with your average size
rearrange my guts & stick the landing

COLORED NAILS

you use colored nails like obama used philosophers

want your hands to be my hands

exploring your body

want to whisper on your mouth

you are so lovely

(heart thief)

what did you say?

i'm over here queering literature

PEN PINEAPPLE APPLE PEN

Ah, models off duty, puking & crying like the rest of us

I explain H-O-R-S-E to Maluma, teach Ricky Martin nursery rhymes

You crib a line from Marie Howe, make a pass at Stacy's Mom

Can't spell Heraclitus without "clit"

You have shit on your sleeve

You're somehow uglier than your manners

Go hang with your chicken cutlets

In this ocean of fuglies

I starve myself to remember how it feels to be satisfied

downward dog pose

Misery loves company but real G's move in silence like lasagna

Down your Shiner Bock, buttery folds of Pillsbury™ Crescent Rolls

IYKYK

Here I am, stone-faced but humming

Quietly assembling this beautiful sandwich

If only I were this regimented abt anything else

I always knew 思念是一种病

I feign liquid courage, watch you recite the 25th Amendment

You, superhuman, dance off the grid

I'll be your parachute, fantasize abt fading out, the last song

But, above all else, wanting you, so desperately,

to stay

POEM IN WHICH THE POET READS THE FORTUNES OF RANDOS

it's october 3rd / i am really tired & your face is greasy / your poems are just long-winded descriptions of what ppl look like / you wish to return as a male model's favorite cat / writing is difficult & stressful but if you do it successfully, you can still be poor! / poets rank slightly below raccoons / i am immigrant i self-publish lichen / you like large boys a queer person / you should write a memoir you have seen some shit / the one you have been seeing is a narc / my legal dream team is jessica rabbit & the cast of modern family / i want our teef to clash yes / peace love boba you are powerless / you are a spinster of 30 / your face is small & thin like a mink's / you think clint eastwood is dead / you would make the beast with two backs for tye sheridan / you live on stolen land / you pretend to like times new roman but your preferred font is garamond / you will be in a horrific accident & will only remember britney lyrics when you wake / you enjoy the golden radiance, the narrow & sculptural flanks of youth / the reports of your attractiveness have been greatly exaggerated / the savageness of your wit has been falsely reported / you will meet the one at new york's hottest club / you sharted at your own birthday party & the smell still lingers / you will fart on a wolf cub & become king / an incident at a wawa once left you scratched & bleeding / you have bedbugs you shall henceforth be known as bedbug girl / you have a sense of inevitability abt dinner / do <u>not</u> trust the "no. <3" crew. they are narcs / there is a special internet for cute ppl & hopefully i will see you there but if not that is fine / you like watching the warmth radiate off him like a spotlight / he will remain unfucked by you / all my endings slap like meat on a counter / back off my bf !!!!

独家记忆 EXCLUSIVE MEMORY

Blake . . . 제발 . . .
我的黑夜比白天多

Spare no expense, don't make me beg
Give me your nine yards, the whole enchilada

As everyone knows
I find it easy to gorge myself

I'll be your 王妃 . . . royal BEAST of BURDEN
You love my empty, my timeshare in Florida

Publish my miraculous words you murderous twink
Are you interesting or are you just from Texas?

~

BOYHOOD KARAOKE

Soulja Boy ahead of his time when he said Kiss Me Thru The Phone

Whiteboy poem: PORTLAND OREGON MAIMED DOG SHOTGUN MY NAZI FRIEND SCARS SKINNED SQURL
Poetry: Congratulations on your acceptance!

Was reading & like Oh! This is good! My own poems—

I don't like too many poetic rules. Mainly b/c I am in my own category

I don't write abt loss b/c Chinese person do not like to lose

I am honored to _____ this generous _____ with such great _____ especially the talented _____

It is actually enormously taxing to congratulate ppl for stuff b/c you could be using that time to eat

My Secret Service code name is Tutti frutti

Read a lot, as much variety as you can, libraries are your friend • Figure out what you don't like & why • Figure out what's left (i.e., what you do like) • What are some sensibilities unique to you? • Sift, mix, match, reason, combine • Arrive at voice. (Gold panning.)

Thank you for spending time with my work but you had nothing going on anyway let's be honest

Replace Likes with Magic 8-Ball answers

I am novice poet created by YouTube & Khan Academy

I am like so buff from eating today

Not with those lewks or line breaks

Jeff Bezos deserves our sympathy he could be even richer think abt it

I'm only asking for niche fame I wish to be famous amongst the queers & fans of fine fragrance

Come for the poetry stay for the insults

What if—for example—I don't like u

Just brag abt urself/ur work WITHOUT the "shameless self promo" bs. We have heard the stories, know of ur shame!

Person: [unrelated topic]
Poets: this is how I came out

The media has a very clear conservative/right-wing bias & anyone who says different is lying

A Very Famous Poet told me that I was "the first Chinese poet (she met) who writes with such teeth"—ya I'm coming for u

I love endings that go M*N ARE UNKIND, WAR IS HERE, PRACTICE SELF-CARE, while my own endings are like BACK OFF MY BF

When they go low you go deep

You can spell my name wrong just start talking abt me—discuss!

Ekphrastic is so hard like what are feelings

I wrote a queer historical poem u wanna talk abt CANON

Advice for you—try harder

Someone's drag name is Sei Shōnagon

Haha CNF writers really stretch to link their banal personal experiences to broader political trends

High school crushes & how they got into Stuyvesant with a dance routine that would now be considered racist

My regular writing practice is going to my bowl & waiting for the food to come

How much more can we read abt hair & body & eyes? Have we not suffered enough

Who among us has not aspired to be a person of consequence

Must scrutinize turkey pardons for fine print pardoning DONALD J. TRUMP, of FLORIDA, for all actual & potential crimes committed June 14, 1946 to infinity

So as to achieve Most Glorious High Engagement, this is Gideon—

Bi boys read & draw hearts in the margins

At the end of my suffering there was an eel that talk too much

I want to start a lit mag called DOUBLE DISINFORMATION

I have a joke abt submissions but I save it for my friends

My poems celebratory & resplendent my voice full of nuance you can say yes

Honestly just tell me when I win

你抽的烟 YOUR CIGARETTE

pocho boy wit the undercut

pick a country

decide u have to have me

cop a look kit & kaboodle

refuse to turn away, a sneeze u can't suppress

my fav thing is how u look brown but sound white

ur flattery worth the same as half-price books

i admit i want to live in a world where u love me

now lie by my side, lazy eye

化成灰我都认得你

SHELF STABLE

"For as the body is one and has many members, but all the members of that one body, being many, are one body, so also is Christ"—1 Corinthians 12:12

"We love disasters that have nothing to do with us"—Mark Doty

●

I have given up on deep-core drillers—
a restaurant I'll never order from again.

As we enter this period of morning business,
how many poems have already been written abt Harvard's glass flowers?

I suppose, like those flowers,
I know absurdity, thrive on abandonment.

I grow, turn into a shack twisting on its very foundations,
rouse in response to your questioning.

Boy with the rifle—
I'll always be the bored child, you'll always be my escape.

Buckle up buttercup—
sex is good, but have you ever fucked the system?

男友视角 BOYFRIEND PERSPECTIVE

ur a honey trap i spot a mile away
> u say *i can't tell if u're actually trying to hurt my feelings*

u know i have a 刀子嘴 • 豆腐心
> i am 好傻好天真

ur a weeklong bacchanal
> i am nervous twirling by myself:

breakfast for dinner
> drink juice at nite

u write the textbook on flirtation
> utilize premium seduction

ur a work of art
> say u will hurt me

i am immune to ur charms
> a pebble in ur shu

u say u need space like a tree
> just make like a tree & leave

u say i give it good
> better than the one in the ground

ur exes don't measure up
> say bye to her say hi to our future

say yes cuz i never been wit an ugly dude
> i bet ur average size is stiff

glow up since high school, i'll give u that
> ur face shine like dawn

remind me 刻板印象
      the kind of boy who went to marist & did okay

ur fish eyes not pearls
      let ur hunger set u free

sometimes it's freeing to love someone
      take off ur life jacket & plunge

A PART VOLATILE

chameleon: put me on a piece of glass
me: [confused]
chameleon: let me be clear …

sometimes i don't know what the fuck i'm doing
lending me the air of a zombie
sending me like *this poem is sending me*
wut witchcraft
transportive bleat of demon sheep
so humble u call me mistress pie

mcqueen tailor galliano art historian
quiet childhood colored pencils the crow of cock
is kim jones kinda stale ??? u look pallid, like u sweat a lot kim
when lee was sewing jackets u were wearing sweatpants
(wut the kaiser called a sign of defeat)
can't recall a kim jones collection standing out the way i can w/ raf (ditto ghesquière)
wut's kim's signature, copycat harnesses ??? reworked saddles ??? daz barely anything
designers burn out, get chewed up by the leviathan,
but dior keeps thriving …

here is our nation
never thought i'd be spilling to strangers
alabaster skin & eyes like pools, no, like glowing stones
u hurt me w/ ur pouty insolence
u talk abt ur family from the old country, their village, i say do u mean the west village ???
it's not advisable to put raw meat on open wounds
ur scent visits me in my sleep wafting up my sorry nostrils rolling in gnawing at me
leaving me panting ur scent so magnanimous & my capacity to register so inadequate
hit me again!

here are the horsemen passing
stampede of foreboding & lament, uniforms starched as fuck
hey sharon olds u have a lot to be sorry for, ur nephews especially
hey sylvia plath ur the best
hey anne sexton who even r u

hey _____ _____ need ur slam, not ur poet
behind every poet: twizzlers & diet coke

here is ur saved-u-a-seat smile
my trusting nature, ur power burrowing in
blurry equestrian paintings, funny once u study them
forgive my mixing metaphors
the wiki for japan's spy agency says it spends
"most of its energy" translating foreign publications rather than gathering intelligence …
page compares it to the cia, claims 170-175 employees (vs the cia's *21,575*)
take ur empire out, let's measure it, we're all losers here
how much time do we spend on useless endeavors, the lies we tell ourselves

here is desire
machine beeping & bopping
knobs & levers awaiting twist or tug
organ seizing, a diabolical hold, severing u from polite intentions
eyes have strayed
pangs of sex endured, ignored
ah! classic misdirection
hard candies & sweet bean paste
tell u wut
kiss me & i'll return the favor, sit gently on u

here is happiness
more or less
what saves us

ACKNOWLEDGMENTS

Dreamers & the people who love me ...

blake levario (♥), the superior poet ...

Evan Trimas ...

My fans ...

My students past, present, & future ...

Lambda Literary, the Poetry Project, & Kundiman, for showing us it can be done ...

The editors at Air/Light, Alien Magazine, Black Warrior Review, Boston Accent Lit, The Broadkill Review, Burrow Press, The Capilano Review, The Cincinnati Review, Clav Mag, Diode Editions, DREGINALD, ellipsis... literature and art, Heavy Feather Review, Honey Literary, Iron Horse Literary Review, The Laurel Review, The Margins (Asian American Writers' Workshop), The Nervous Breakdown, No Contact Mag, The Puritan, Sidereal Magazine, Sporklet (Spork Press), Swamp Ape Review, The Tangerine, & Volume Poetry for their great selections ...

And, of course, immeasurable gratitude to Barracuda Guarisco at Really Serious Literature ...

MICHAEL CHANG (they/them) is the author of DRAKKAR NOIR, winner of the Bateau Press BOOM Chapbook Contest, as well as CHINATOWN ROMEO (Ursus Americanus Press, 2021). Tapped to edit Lambda Literary's Emerge anthology, their poems have been nominated for Best New Poets, Best of the Net, & the Pushcart Prize. In 2021, they were awarded the Poetry Project's prestigious Brannan Prize.

CPSIA information can be obtained
at www.ICGtesting.com
Printed in the USA
BVHW051004201221
624256BV00004B/78